Robert Tressell, Dubliner
Author of
The Ragged Trousered Philanthropists

I ndilchuimhne ar mo mháthair
Máire Nic Mhathúna (1920-2013)

Robert Tressell, Dubliner
Author of
The Ragged Trousered Philanthropists

To Brendan

Bryan MacMahon

Bryan MacMahon

ISBN: 978-0-9549865-8-2

Email: tresselldublin@gmail.com

Profits from the sale of this book will go to Barnardos

Published by
KILMACUD STILLORGAN LOCAL HISTORY SOCIETY
www.kilmacudstillorganhistory.ie

Design by
ASHFIELD PRESS, 30 LINDEN GROVE, BLACKROCK, CO. DUBLIN
www.ashfieldpress.ie

Printed by
GRAPH PRINT, A9 CALMOUNT PARK, DUBLIN 12

Contents

ROBERT
TRESSELL
born Robert Noonan
socialist,
painter, signwriter
and author of
"The Ragged Trousered
Philanthropists"
18th april 1870 –
– 3rd february 1911

Plaque at No.37 Wexford St.,
Dublin.

Introduction

WHEN KATHLEEN NOONAN sold the rights to her father's manuscript in 1913, she could not have imagined that the book would become internationally famous, would never be out of print for a century and would be published as a World Classic by Oxford University Press in 2005. Nor could she have expected that a street in Dublin would have a memorial to her father. The plaque over the door of No.37 Wexford Street is somewhat lost amid the clutter of signs on that busy thoroughfare and few passers-by notice it. The fading inscription reads: "Robert Tressell, born Robert Noonan, socialist, painter, sign-writer and author of *The Ragged Trousered Philanthropists*. 18th April 1870 – 3rd February 1911."

Robert Noonan took his pen-name from the trestle table which was part of his equipment as a painter-decorator. *The Ragged Trousered Philanthropists* (*RTP*) was his only book and it was completed in 1910 when he lived in Hastings in East Sussex, after his return from Cape Town in 1901. The manuscript of almost 1,700 pages was initially rejected by three publishers and Robert was on the point of burning it but Kathleen persuaded him not to. He died within a year of completing his book and never saw it in print.

Often unable to work due to ill-health, he had devoted all his energy over several years to his semi-autobiographical novel, adding this revealing note on the title page: "Being the story of twelve months in Hell, told by one of the damned." His health had always been frail and he had symptoms of tuberculosis. After his failure to secure a publisher, a disillusioned Robert Noonan travelled alone to Liverpool hoping to find work and secure passage to Canada to make a new start there with his daughter. However, he was taken ill and died on 3rd February 1911 in the Liverpool Royal Infirmary, which was the workhouse hospital. The cause of his death was "cardiac arrest due to phthisis or pulmonary tuberculosis." He was laid to rest in an unmarked pauper's grave nearby.

This man of three countries – Ireland, South Africa and England – has left his mark on social history with a highly influential book and had a life story that is fascinating and perplexing. He lived in five towns or cities which have celebrated their association with him, but Hastings (called "Mugsborough" in the novel) has a pre-eminent place. In Liverpool, there is an annual commemoration at his graveside, and he was specifically honoured there in 2011, the centenary of his death. His time in Cape Town and Johannesburg has been documented in biographies. However, Dublin has been slower to recognise his achievement, although the simple Wexford Street plaque and another in Dublin Writers Museum ensure that he is not entirely forgotten.

The first edition (in an abbreviated and expurgated form) of *The Ragged Trousered Philanthropists* appeared on 23rd April 1914, and this book is published to mark the centenary. It is intended to bring Robert Tressell's astonishing achievement to the attention of more Irish readers and to add to the little information already known about his Irish background. While Robert's childhood and early manhood remain mysterious, a great deal of new information about the lives of his parents, Mary Noonan and Samuel Croker, has been discovered.

Robert Noonan c. 1908.
(Trades Union Congress Library Collections, London Metropolitan University.)

As part of the research for the book, family historian Fíona Tipple traced the Croker/Noonan records and made many surprising discoveries. Another dramatic development came on 14th February 2014, when Brenda Douglas, a descendant of Robert Noonan's sister Ellie, found that Robert was living in London at the time of the 1881 census. He was named in the census return as living at No.27 Elmore Street, Finsbury, with his mother Mary, step-father Sebastian Zumbuhl and two half-brothers, Sebastian and Leo. His age is given as nine, when he was in fact eleven. This dramatic revelation that Robert Noonan was living in London in 1881 means that all previous speculation about his early life and influences must be revised. Since it came as this book was about to go to print, some speculation here now also needs revision. The astonishing discovery is explained in more detail at the end of Chapter 10. I am grateful to Brenda for sharing this new information.

WHO WAS ROBERT TRESSELL? His two principal biographers have chapters headed with this question of identity: F. C. Ball in his book *One of the Damned: The Life and Times of Robert Tressell, author of 'The Ragged Trousered Philanthropists'* (1973) and Dave Harker in *Tressell: The Real Story of 'The Ragged Trousered Philanthropists'* (2003). Robert Noonan was born in No.37 Wexford St. in Dublin on 18th April 1870 and it is believed he left home around the age of 16, eventually reaching South Africa by 1890, when he was 20. Little is known for certain about Robert between the registration of his birth on 18th April 1870 and the registration of his marriage in Cape Town in 1891, but it has been assumed that he lived in Ireland for most, if not all, of this formative period. He is recorded in Cape Town in 1891 working as a painter-decorator and he moved to Johannesburg around 1896. In a document of 1897 he stated that Ireland was his last country of residence.

In the 1890s, Cape Town was booming, with many male, white, single men coming to work there. Robert worked as a skilled artisan and painter, occasionally contributing articles to local newspapers. Unfortunately, none of these writings has survived or been identified, except the title of one article: "All meals a shilling." It is possible that he used a pen-name.

MARRIAGE AND DIVORCE

Robert married Elizabeth Hartel on 15th October 1891 in the Church of the Holy Trinity, Cape Town, a Protestant church. His name is recorded as Robert Phillipe Noonan and his age is given as twenty-three (when he was actually twenty-one) and Elizabeth was eighteen. Little is known about Elizabeth, but the surname indicates that she may have been an Afrikaner. Robert's address was No.78 Strand Street, Cape Town. His profession was described as "decorator". A daughter, Kathleen, was born in September 1892 in the suburb of Mowbray in Cape Town. The marriage was unhappy and ended in divorce, leaving Robert with custody of Kathleen. Records of the divorce case of 1897 survive, with Robert as plaintiff. He declared that the marriage had been "reasonably happy" for about three years. When he moved to Johannesburg Elizabeth joined him intermittently, returning to Cape Town on several occasions. There are no further records of Elizabeth after the divorce.

It was in Johannesburg that Robert was first introduced to labour politics and trade union activism. In 1897 he was Secretary of the Transvaal Federated Building Trades Council and, ironically in light of his later beliefs, one his earliest acts was to protest against the employment of black skilled labour. He attended a meeting to launch the International Independent Labour Party in May 1899, and was elected to the committee. According to Professor Jonathan Hyslop, Johannesburg had grown "from a tented mining camp to a city of over 100,000 people" and was "already an international by-word for greed, commercial swindles and wanton disregard for human life."

Kathleen moved to Johannesburg to be with her father and boarded at a Catholic convent school. She was well cared for there, having her own nurse. She had weekly Sunday visits from Robert, which she and other children enjoyed because he brought treats and played games with them.

Many years later Stuart Ogilvy recorded his warm recollections of Robert's time in South Africa, describing him as "a very good sign-writer indeed .... with the makings of a brilliant artist." He was "an interesting and entertaining companion .... who lived in a world of his own, and was very fond of writing, especially articles about everyday life". Ogilvy recalled that Robert spent a lot of time writing a book about his impressions of the people of Johannesburg. When he later read *RTP*, Ogilvy said that he had no difficulty in "identifying some of the characters portrayed as being derived from some of the oddities Noonan had subjected to such close examination and study during the years he lived on the Rand."

Robert and Kathleen in Cape Town
c. 1896.
(Trades Union Congress Library
Collections, London Metropolitan
University.)

He described Robert's appearance:

> Noonan was short and well-built. We used to call him 'little Noonan'. He walked with a sharp energetic step and a slight roll or sway. His speech was good and accent very slightly Irish. He did not mix much with the others but on the whole he was a good little chap. He always had an eye for queer characters, and he would follow them about endlessly listening to their conversations and taking voluminous notes of how they looked and what they said.

1798 CENTENARY COMMEMORATION

Robert had steady work with the painting and decorating firm of Herbert Evans, and he was reasonably well paid, rising to the position of foreman. As well as being involved in trade union activities, he was active in political affairs and he moved in Irish circles. In 1898 he became a member of the Executive Committee of the Transvaal 1798 Commemoration Committee, part of an international resurgence of Irish nationalism. Robert's membership card of the Transvaal Executive has survived, with his signature, R. P. Noonan.

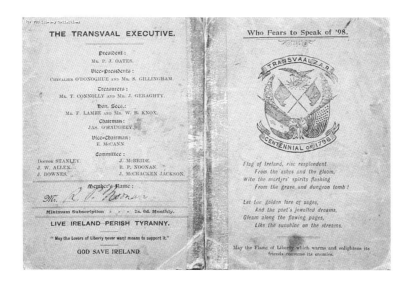

Robert Noonan's signed membership card of the Transvaal Executive of the Centennial 1798 Committee. (Trades Union Congress Library Collections, London Metropolitan University.)

Another member of that executive was an Irish nationalist named John MacBride who worked as an assayer for the Rand Mining Corporation. He was also promoting the cause of Irish separatism in South Africa, an attempt to internationalise the movement for Irish independence. About six thousand Irish people lived in South Africa at the time, most of them ambitious and enterprising young men. MacBride and many others identified with the Boers in their fight against the mighty British Empire. He went on to be executed in Dublin as a leader of the 1916 Rising. MacBride's friend, Arthur Griffith, joined him in South Africa for a short time, from 1897 to 1899. He was primarily a journalist and later, back in Dublin, the founder of Sinn Féin; it is very likely that he and Noonan would have met in the same nationalist circles in Johannesburg. Both MacBride and Griffith went to South Africa for health reasons mainly, but they had been members of nationalist cultural movements in Dublin before they left, and they continued their political activities among the Irish in South Africa. Griffith was editor of a newspaper called the *Middelburg Courant,* but his support for the Boer cause alienated his English readers and the newspaper folded. Back in Ireland, Griffith continued his publishing and political activities, and eventually became first President of Dáil Éireann, the Irish parliament. He died in 1922.

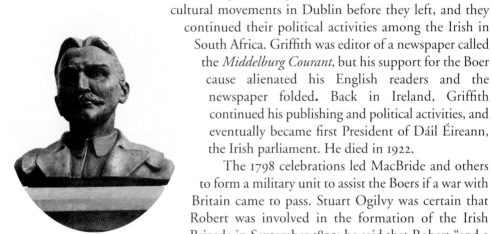

Memorial to Major John MacBride in Westport, Co. Mayo.

The 1798 celebrations led MacBride and others to form a military unit to assist the Boers if a war with Britain came to pass. Stuart Ogilvy was certain that Robert was involved in the formation of the Irish Brigade in September 1899; he said that Robert "and a lot of other wild Irishmen used regularly to meet and concert their plans." However, Robert's involvement ended there and he did not take any part in military activities. The Irish Brigade fought with the Boers when the war broke out in October 1899 and Major John MacBride, as second in command, earned a reputation as a very able military leader. This made him a hero when he returned to Ireland with the unique record among nationalist leaders of having actually taken up arms against the British Empire. Although he was not part of the planning of the 1916 Rising in Dublin, MacBride was invited to become involved at the last minute, which he did. For that reason, and because his military reputation was known to the authorities, he was executed with the other leaders.

It is likely that the reason why Robert did not join the Boer conflict was because he was a single man and the sole carer of a young daughter, with more pressing responsibilities than the other men. Also, he was out of work in the autumn of 1899, as the firm of Herbert Evans had closed down, and there would have been no pay in the Irish Brigade. His chest and lung problems may also have been a factor. In October 1899, shortly before Boer War broke out,

Robert left Johannesburg for Cape Town, travelling on an open truck in overcrowded conditions. The journey took three days and three nights in weather conditions that did not help his health. He told Kathleen that his health problems were caused by "drinking whisky to keep warm when riding across the veldt at night, and getting chilled." He would later jokingly refer to himself as "One Lung" a Chinaman.

DEPARTURE FROM SOUTH AFRICA

Robert's sister Mrs. Adelaide Rolleston, whose husband had worked with the British Consulate in Santiago, Chile, had been recently widowed, and Robert invited her to join him in Cape Town. Adelaide had a young son named Arthur, and it seems that Robert saw them as forming a family unit which would be good for the two children. He sent Adelaide the money to join him, and she travelled via England, spending some time with her sister in Hastings. Robert was obliged to send her more money to enable her to complete the journey, indicating that he had a good standard of living in South Africa and had savings to draw on. Records show that he owned a plot of land, a house site, and the two adults with their children lived in Rondebosch, a middle class suburb of Cape Town. In 1901, however, Robert and Adelaide decided to move to England, first to London and then to "dear sunny Hastings" at the invitation of their sister, Mary Jane. When they first went to Hastings they were briefly joined by another sister, Ellie, who lived in Liverpool. This re-union of the four siblings was not to be repeated.

Robert had a mischievous streak, as revealed in some anecdotes which survive about his time in South Africa. In the custom of expatriates of those times, he had a servant or houseboy in Johannesburg who was named Sixpence. The only item that Sixpence ever stole from Robert was the emerald-green sash of the United Irishmen, which he would have worn at the centenary celebrations. Robert was said to have relished the image of Sixpence parading in front of his wives wearing only his loincloth and the green sash. Incredibly, while on the voyage to England on the *SS*

Kathleen Noonan.
(Trades Union Congress Library Collections, London Metropolitan University.)

13

Galician (a ship built in Belfast by Harland and Wolff), Robert produced a hand-written news bulletin entitled *The Evening Ananias* for distribution among passengers, writing under the pseudonym "George Washington." No copies have survived. He also played a practical joke by wetting his sister's fur stole and putting it in a passenger's bed, making it look like an animal.

HASTINGS

Robert Noonan lived in Hastings from 1901 to 1910. His sister Mary Jane ran a school for the blind in the town; her daughter Alice was blind. Her husband, John Bean Meiklejon, lived in London most of the time. For the first four years Robert and Kathleen continued to share lodgings with Adelaide and Arthur, and they had several changes of address in that period. From 1906 father and daughter were on their own, living at various addresses in the town. Robert had been a father to Arthur and undoubtedly the separation was painful; it seems that tensions arose because Adelaide disapproved of Robert's political activism and his atheism. Arthur joined the army and was killed in the Great War. The last address of Robert and Kathleen was 241 London Road, St. Leonard's, a prosperous suburb of Hastings, from late 1907 or early 1908, and it was there that Robert completed his magnum opus, *RTP*.

Hastings was widely known from the historical association of the Battle of 1066, and was a typical southern coastal seaside town, with its fashionable pier and a reputation as a health resort, a suitable setting for a man with chest and lung problems. It had a population of approximately 65,000 people and had no major industries; employment was mainly in the service areas. Fred Ball described it as follows: "The town being entirely without factories and industry, the working classes lived off the Corporation (and men literally fought for jobs

Two views of Hastings in the early 1900s. (Steve Peak)

there), the public utilities, the railways (and horse-buses), shops and hotels (the two worst-paid occupations), and domestic service, or the 'kiss-me-Aunt' trades as they were referred to....... And last of all was the building."

Robert found a position fairly quickly with Bruce and Co., Electrical and Sanitary Engineers and Builders, working as a skilled interior decorator. Moving from self-employed status in South Africa to employee status in Hastings had an effect on him, although his talent was recognised because he was paid the top rate of 7½ pence an hour for a working week of at least fifty-six hours. Kathleen went to a boarding school in Deal, Kent and to the Convent of the Sacred Heart in Hastings. In 1904, she moved to a free Church of England school and three years later she won a bursary to another school.

Robert disliked the foreman in Bruce and Co. who was probably one model for the despised foreman Hunter/Nimrod/Misery in the novel. He may have spent some time in London after leaving Bruce. In 1902-3, he moved to Burton and Co. Builders, Contractors, Decorators and Funeral Directors, where his work involved painting, gilding and graining. He was also occasionally called on to inscribe coffin plates and sign-writing was another of his skills. Fred Ball met some people who remembered Robert in Hastings, in particular a young apprentice named William Gower, who was in awe of Robert and recalled many details of their experience.

Robert Noonan was small and dapper, five-feet three-inches in height and nine stone in weight. His friends in Hastings knew him as Bob and nicknamed him "the professor". He was widely read and had an extensive collection of books which he used as a lending library for friends. The library included weighty tomes by Plutarch, Pliny, Plato and Gibbon but he also read Conan Doyle and Bram Stoker. According to Kathleen, Robert spoke several languages, and she specified French, German, Dutch, Italian, Spanish and Gaelic. He dressed well and wore a trilby to work rather than the soft hat worn by his fellows. On Sundays he wore a grey suit and soft hat and sported a walking stick. He drank in moderation, enjoyed cricket and took Kathleen to operatic performances. Surprisingly, he does not seem to have been a member of a trade union while in Hastings.

Robert was also short-tempered and inclined to be combative with superiors. In one of several confrontations with authority, he locked his employer into a room after being called a blackguard. He had one costly brush with the law in Hastings, over a relatively trivial matter. He distributed some fireworks to children in November 1905 and was outraged when a man approached the children, caught one of them roughly and took the firework from him. Robert got involved and challenged the man, who turned out to be a policeman in plain clothes. The law did not allow children to play with fireworks in public and Robert was convicted of obstructing a policeman, fined 10 shillings and obliged to pay £1. 9 shillings costs. This was a severe financial penalty.

A fragment of Robert
Noonan's work on St.
Andrew's Church survives
in Hastings Museum.
(Robert Tressell Society)

Only very little of the work done by Robert in Hastings survived. He worked on St. Andrew's Church, renovating the chancel in elaborate style. This was completed for Easter 1905 and was the gift of Robert's employer, Mr. Burton, to the church. Unfortunately, St. Andrew's was demolished in 1970, but thanks to the alertness of Fred Ball and others, some examples of his original work were preserved and are now on display in Hastings Museum. After this job, his workmates dubbed him "Raphael." From September 1903 to June 1904, Robert and many members of Burton's staff worked on the renovation of a house named Val Mescal, and this is believed to have been the model for the house called "The Cave" in *RTP*, where the central characters spend the year at work.

AIRSHIPS AND MAGIC LANTERNS

In his early days in Hastings, Robert was not involved in politics and his interest was focussed instead on developments in flight. He took a great interest in airships and around 1902 he wrote an article entitled "The Evolution of the Airship." This was probably intended for publication and was accompanied by Robert's own drawings of early balloons and airships. Apart from a letter to his daughter, this article and *RTP* are the only examples of Robert's writings which survived.

The subject of flight was a topical one in the early 1900s, and Robert's article described the Zeppelin airship, which made its trial flight in June 1900. He ended his article with a long reference to "the dirigible balloon which Dr. Barton is building for the British government..... a distinct advance on any of its predecessors known to the general public." The age-old problem with balloon flight since the days of the earliest experiments of the 1780s was that balloons were completely subject to the winds and could not be steered or directed. Robert concluded his article: "It has been demonstrated beyond question that it is possible to construct dirigible balloons which can be driven in any desired direction on calm days."

Such was Robert's interest in aviation that he built a model airship in his garden, with help from his young friend, Bill Gower. It was six feet long and had three pairs of three-bladed propellers with a rudder at the rear. It was named "Martian" and was "manned" by little doll figures. It was painted all over in aluminium and decorated in red, green and gold with a flag at the rear which carried the emblem of the harp of Ireland. Some accounts say that Robert submitted the airship for a competition and that he offered the design to the War Office, but nothing came of these and Gower says that he finally smashed it up with a hammer.

Gower also recalled another venture with Robert. Together they attempted to make a little money by setting up a travelling magic lantern show, grandiosely titled The South Coast Amusement Company. It was Robert's idea and they hired a set of slides called "A Trip around the World" to show in village halls. The plan was that Gower would show the slides and Robert would give the lecture. It proved to be a short-lived experiment – they travelled by bicycle to a village called Brede, and entertained a full house, but the long, late return journey in wet conditions put Robert off ever repeating it. In another burst of enthusiasm Robert had a plan for showing moving pictures in a hall on the pier, but Gower was not keen and the plan was dropped. To their chagrin, another man soon afterwards did successfully set up film shows on the pier.

POLITICAL ACTIVISM

In the general election of January 1906, the Liberals had a sweeping success all over the country, but in Hastings the Conservative candidate gained the seat, against the national pattern. He was an Irishman, (William) Harvey du Cros, an entrepreneur who controlled the Dunlop Tyre Company. Two years later he suddenly resigned on health grounds and in the by-election the seat was won by his son, Arthur, who was born in Dublin. Election affairs feature prominently in *RTP*, with the Conservative candidate named satirically as Sir Graball D'Encloseland.

The year 1906 also marks Robert's entry into political affairs in the town. In September, a meeting was held in The Cricketers pub to form the Social Democratic Federation (SDF) with Robert, Alf Cobb and Edward Cruttenden involved. Cruttenden lived near Robert and the two families became friendly. The SDF was a Marxist organisation, first established in 1884, and it was more radical that the newly formed Labour Party.

These interests led to conflict between Robert and his sisters, and ultimately Adelaide and Arthur moved out to live elsewhere in the town. Despite the years of shared accommodation with Adelaide and the invitation to come to Hastings from Mary Jane, the three were not very close and some of the bitterness towards Robert is apparent in these comments of Alice, his niece, to Fred Ball:

> I saw little of him but I knew his extreme socialist opinions. He had always been extremely vehement and very, very bitter. We believed this to be partly temperamental (self-willed, headstrong, idealistic, high-principled etc) and partly the disappointment and disillusionment of his early life, though, of course, his intellectual power and strong sympathies would naturally incline him to socialism.

In late 1906, Robert left the firm of Burton and Co., possibly after some conflicts, including a reprimand over taking too long on a job. He went to work for the prominent firm of Adams and Jarrett in St. Leonard's. Robert's sign-writing skills were put to work on an elaborate gable advertisement for the company which survived until it was painted over in the 1960s. It measured 30ft by 25ft and a photograph of it is the only record.

An example of Robert Noonan's sign-writing. He is at bottom right, wearing hat.
(Steve Peak)

During 1907, Robert was deeply involved in the affairs of the SDF, writing manifestos, making banners, distributing leaflets, collecting donations and speaking at public meetings. He was a poor speaker and on one occasion, when a man insulted the red flag, Robert was furious and chased him along the beach. There was an economic downturn at this time in England and building workers were being laid-off, leading to great hardship for some families. A soup kitchen was in operation in Hastings in 1909 and the town's workhouse was filled to capacity.

By 1908, Robert had withdrawn somewhat from public campaigning and it is believed that he spent the years 1908 and 1909 completing his manuscript, possibly from notes already made over the years, and he finished it in early 1910. The title page read as follows: *The Ragged Trousered Philanthropists, being the story of twelve months in Hell, told by one of the damned and written down by Robert Tressell.* It has been speculated that Robert's preferred title may have been *The Ragged-Arsed Philanthropists* and that he realised that this title could not be used. "Ragged-arsed" was a familiar colloquialism among the workers, and "ragged trousered" would have been was "a prissy phrase" to them, according to Fred Ball. Robert sent the manuscript to three publishers in 1910, only to have it rejected by all three. In despair, he wanted to burn the

Kathleen Noonan.
(Trades Union Congress Library Collections, London Metropolitan University.)

manuscript but Kathleen persuaded him not to. He stored it in a metal box which he had made himself and there it stayed.

During the winter of 1909-10, Robert's health was noticeably worsening and he had regular absences from work. "He always looked cold and pinched looking, as if he needed a good meal," said one of his friends. Kathleen remembered that "he would have recurrent attacks of bronchitis and would cough and cough." Although they were short of money, he would sometimes give her a few shillings for what he sardonically called "riotous living" and he was pleased to see her good examination results.

In August 1910, Robert left for Liverpool, apparently planning to earn the fare for him and Kathleen to move to Canada and make a new beginning. He would seem to have had a belief that a change of location could solve his problems. He told none of his friends and acquaintances of his plan and he said no farewells. Kathleen stayed in Hastings with her aunt Mary Jane, and her father promised to return for her when travel arrangements to Canada were made. They parted at Hastings railway station and were never to meet again.

DEATH IN LIVERPOOL

Robert spent the autumn and winter of 1910 in Liverpool but very little is known about his time there and there is no evidence of any contact with his sister Ellie, who lived in the city. In November he was admitted to the Royal Infirmary (the workhouse hospital) and he wrote to Kathleen saying that he was quite happy and decorating the ward for Christmas. He had always had a fear of ending up in the workhouse and he was most likely trying to reassure Kathleen of his welfare. For her part, she was accustomed to him being ill and was not unduly worried about his condition.

Adams and Jarrett, Hastings, where Robert worked. (Steve Peak)

Robert Noonan died on 3rd February 1911 and Kathleen received a telegram saying simply "Your father died at 10.15 last night." At 18, she had no independent means and was in the care of her aunt Mary Jane; neither she nor any of Robert's family travelled to Liverpool. Mary Jane advised Kathleen to instruct the hospital authorities to "make the usual arrangements." Robert was buried in an unmarked grave in the nearby cemetery, along with twelve other paupers.

A fragment of a letter from Robert to Kathleen survives, written soon after he left Hastings in August 1910. He assured her of his love, apologised for his unkindness and irritability towards her, which he said was caused by worries, and ended:

> I have thought of nothing but you since I lost sight of you on the platform and the world seems a dreary place to me because you are not here. I cannot write down here all that I feel and want to say to you but if it were true that circumstances compelled us to live apart from each other permanently then I would much prefer not to continue at all. *Je vous aime toujours*, Dad.

Robert was a devoted and loving father. This letter, his long manuscript and a short essay on airships are the sum total of the writings left by him. Little did he or Kathleen realise in 1910 that a hundred years later his novel would be widely read and admired. Dave Harker speculates that Robert may have left Hastings out of a desire to spare his loved ones the experience of seeing him going to the workhouse there. Fear of ending up in the workhouse looms large among the workers in the novel, and one man, Jack Linden, dies a lonely death there.

2 First publication of *RTP* in 1914

AFTER ROBERT'S DEATH in 1911 at the age of forty, Kathleen at first stayed with her aunt helping at the school for the blind. Then she moved to London where her first cousin Paul Meiklejon lived, and they became romantically involved. He was an actor and Kathleen worked as a nurse-governess with a family named Mckinlay. On one occasion the Mckinlays had a visitor named Jessie Pope who was a journalist, a poet and writer of children's books and a contributor to *Punch* magazine. Kathleen told her she had the manuscript of a novel in her room and asked Miss Pope to read it. "I consented without enthusiasm," wrote Jessie Pope, "expecting to be neither interested nor amused – and found I had chanced upon a remarkable human document."

Pope recommended it to a friend in publishing, Thomas Franklin Grant Richards, whose reaction to what he called "that mountainous manuscript" was that "the book was damnably subversive but it was extraordinarily real." Both agreed that it was worth publishing but would have to be edited first. Pope thought that it was "ever and ever so much too long; full of repetition. It would have to be cut down." Grant Richards proposed to buy the manuscript outright and offered Kathleen £25 for all rights to it. She was earning £12 a year at the time so she readily accepted this offer, which surpassed all her expectations.

Kathleen resisted suggestions that the title should be changed, and although Richards and Pope discussed alternative titles such as *The Ragged Philanthropists*, *The Tattered Philanthropists* and *The Threadbare Philanthropists*, they retained Tressell's original. For some reason, Pope however did change the spelling of Tressell to Tressall. That form of the surname was on all editions of the book up to 1955.

Was Kathleen exploited? It has been argued that it was a generous price for a book on an unpopular subject matter by an unknown dead author, and that it was a risk for the publisher. Frank Swinnerton wrote that copyright was often sold for less, and that "even an author destined to become a best-seller would have been pleased to begin so well." Jessie Pope also believed that Kathleen was treated well, and wrote: "I don't think that anybody could read that manuscript and treat the daughter of the man who wrote it badly."

Pope accepted Grant Richards' invitation to edit the book for publication and she received £24 as a fee. She cut out over one-third of the text, omitting scenes and language deemed to be vulgar or offensive and cutting the original fifty-four chapters to thirty-six, from 250,000 words to 150,000. The first edition was published on 23rd April 1914, three years after Robert's death. Two thousand copies were printed and it sold at 6 shillings. Only Kathleen and the publishers were aware that it was an abridged version of Tressell's manuscript.

Plaque at No.241 London Road. (Steve Peak)

A Hastings scene, c. 1908. (Steve Peak)

KATHLEEN NOONAN IN CANADA

After the publication of the book, Kathleen made the decision to leave England for Canada where Paul Meiklejon had already settled. They married and worked on the stage as part of a touring theatre company. Their daughter Joan was born in 1915. Around 1919, word came back from Paul to relatives that Kathleen and Joan had been killed in a car crash. So it appeared that this tragedy brought the Noonan/Tressell line to an end. Apart from Grant Richards and Jessie Pope, there were few others who knew the story of the origins of the book which had become so popular. Sales continued to be healthy, with all rights in the hands of the publisher Grant Richards, and information on its mysterious author was scanty.

PLOT OUTLINE

The novel is set in the town of Mugsborough, a version of Hastings. It centres on a group of workers who are renovating a house which is called "The Cave" and the main character is Frank Owen. The pen-name Tressell was Robert's way of protecting his identity, as he feared victimisation from employers. It comes from the word trestle, a table with folding legs used by painters and workmen.

Frank Owen is arrogant, impatient and idealistic, and is frustrated by the inertia and servility of his fellow workers, whom he urges to aspire to better lives and to challenge the system which keeps them in subservience. Owen is also compassionate and generous, but he is not popular. Another character is Barrington (who was completely omitted from the 1914 edition) who turns out to come from a well-to-do background. Owen and Barrington represent the beliefs of the author, with the latter giving lectures on socialism.

The odd title of the book comes from a passage in which Owen is infuriated by the docility of his workmates and he voices some vitriolic attacks on their gullibility, fatalism and apathy. Old Jack Linden sums up the attitudes of his fellow workers: "Things can't never be haltered. There's always been rich and poor in the world and there always will be." Owen's response is as follows:

> As Owen thought of his child's future, there sprang up within him a feeling of hatred and fury at his fellow workmen – they were the enemy, those ragged trousered philanthropists who not only quietly submitted like so many cattle to their miserable slavery for the benefit of others, but defended it and opposed and ridiculed any suggestion of reform. They were the real oppressors – the men who spoke of themselves as "the likes of us", who having lived in poverty all their lives considered that what had been good enough for them was good enough for their children.

This passage is the origin of the book's title. Jessie Pope's Preface in 1914 stressed the authenticity of the book's descriptions of working class life and work and showed that she was impressed by the power of the book:

> With grim humour and pitiless realism, the working man has revealed the lives and hearts of his mates, their opinion of their betters, their political views, their attitudes towards Socialism. Through the busy din of the hammer and the scraping knife, the clang of the pail, the swish of the whitewash, the yell of the foreman, comes the talk of the men, their jokes and curses, their hopes and terrors, the whimpering of their old people, the cry of their children.

Pope made light of the changes she made to the original:

> In reducing a large mass of manuscript to the limitations of book form, it has been my task to cut away superfluous matter and repetition only. The rest practically remains as it came from the pen of Robert Tressall, house-painter and sign-writer who recorded his criticism of the present scheme of things, until weary of the struggle, he slipped out of it.

It was very important to Pope that Tressell was himself a working class writer and she depicts him as enduring great adversity. Her alterations and omissions included a rape scene, lectures on socialism, vulgarities and coarseness, and above all the changing of the ending. Instead of the optimistic ending of Tressell's manuscript, which looked forward to the establishment of "the Co-operative Commonwealth," she ends the 1914 version with a passage in which Owen anticipates his own death and considers the murder of his wife and young child as a solution to his concerns for their future. The last sentences of Pope's edition of the book were: "If he could not give them happiness, he could at least put them out of the reach of further suffering. If he could not stay and protect them, it would

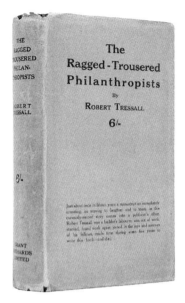

First edition of *The Ragged Trousered Philanthropists*, 1914. (Wikipedia)

be kinder and more merciful to take them with him." This change from Tressell's ending was one that deeply offended readers when it eventually became known.

FIRST REVIEWS

In the first three months after publication 1,752 copies were sold in Britain, 250 in Canada and 1,400 in other colonies. There were many reviews in the press and most were favourable. Tressell was compared with another Irish writer of the time, Patrick McGill, whose book about the hard lives of young Irish emigrants in Scotland, *Children of the Dead End,* appeared at around the same time.

"Slowly the workers are becoming articulate", wrote one reviewer; "the new workman is a rebel .... not willing to put up with the hardship and privations ... which the old workman accepted as necessary evils." Another wrote: "There is no-one, no-one at all, who will be after reading it, quite the same man as he was before. No commendation of this book can be exaggerated." In *The Times,* the reviewer wrote: "The book lives by its minute fidelity, its convincing air of fact and by the writer's passion for his subject. He had a remarkable gift for the suggestion of character. Before the tale is over, we know every one of these working men so well that we should recognise them in the street. .."

The *Daily Sketch* declared it "a wonderful book and Robert Tressall must have been a wonderful man, for he was but a house-painter himself. Formless and without a connected story, it can hardly be called a novel. It is rather a series of character studies, conversations and incidents depicted with the minute exactitude that Tolstoy employed."

Criticisms of the book were that it had "the faults of a tract" and "a suspicious resemblance to propagandist pamphlets." One journalist noted "a lack of skill in story-telling and construction" and was "continually distracted by the wish that the author had been a genius."

The Penguin edition of 1940
(Board of Trinity College)

Just a few months after the publication of *RTP*, the Great War broke out and socialists in all countries rallied to their national cause. All book sales collapsed and there was little interest in socialist themes. But in 1915 this chance remark from a Scottish book dealer about *RTP* was reported to Grant Richards: "Now there's a book I could sell any number of." Grant Richards saw an opening for another edition and began to prepare it, again edited by Jessie Pope. This was published in May 1918 and was abridged even more than the 1914 edition, to 90,000 words. It was targeted at working-class readers and it sold at one shilling. By 1932 it had been reprinted eight times and over 100,000 copies had been sold. In 1940, Penguin published the 1918 edition and, as it sold at sixpence, it reached a wide readership. The 1940 edition was misleadingly described as "complete and unabridged."

1914-1955

From 1914 until its publication in full in 1955, *RTP* attracted many readers and was enormously influential. It won over many converts to socialism, with sales influenced by the events of the time, for example, the great strike of 1926, the depression of the 1930s, the rise of Communism in Russia, and the growth of the Labour Party. Dave Harker's *Tressell* gives a comprehensive account of the fortunes of the novel in relation to British and world politics.

During World War Two the book circulated very widely among the troops. It was passed from reader to reader, with encouragement from the publishers who had this inscription on it: "For the Forces. Leave this book at any Post

Office when you have read it so that men and women in the services may enjoy it too." This custom continued for years and many people first learned of the book while they were in the forces. The novel, known familiarly as *RTP*, or "The Ragged", has since become "a working-class classic", and has sold well over a million copies in at least ten languages. It has been called "the socialist bible" and "a working-class Vanity Fair." The Penguin first printing of 50,000 copies in 1940 sold out within a month, a rate of over one copy every minute, as Harker points out. These were the circumstances which led to the claim that was *RTP* was the book which won the 1945 election for Labour, by winning over many supporters to the policies of the party.

It was regularly given to apprentices in Ireland as well as in Britain as a kind of manual when they began to serve their time, and it converted many to socialism. Its characters became widely known in the trades and "Misery" was the nickname given to many foremen on building sites. Painters and decorators have a special appreciation for *RTP* because it described their lives and conditions, because Tressell was one of their own and because Frank Owen was described as secretary of the Painters' Union. However, it is surprising that trade unions are barely mentioned in the book.

3 Fred Ball's quest

Frederick Cyril Ball worked as a meter-reader with the Gas Company in Hastings and when he first read *The Ragged Trousered Philanthropists* in 1935 he became fascinated. Fred Ball came from a working-class background and his grandfather was a tradesman in Hastings at the time when the novel was set. In the early 1940s Fred began to research the life of Robert Tressell and most of what we now know of his time in South Africa and in Hastings is thanks to this research. Fred corresponded with people who knew Robert in South Africa and collected anecdotes from people who knew him in Hastings. He also received information from Alice Meiklejon, daughter of Mary Jane and sister of Paul. Ball began to write Tressell's biography in 1946-47 and it was published by Lawrence and Wishart in 1951 under the title *Tressell of Mugsborough*. Ball wrote it "for the rank and file worker" and the book sold well. The information available to Ball at that time was inaccurate and incomplete and he went on to publish a revised book, *One of The Damned*, in 1973.

THE DISCOVERY OF THE MANUSCRIPT

There were many dramatic breakthrough moments in Fred Ball's on-going quest for details of Tressell's life and death. The first of these came in the course of his correspondence with Grant Richards on the subject of the manuscript. Grant Richards confirmed that the manuscript was in existence and was in the hands of a man who might indeed be willing to sell it for the 'modest sum' of about £50, as proposed by Ball. Negotiations were intermittent and in November 1945, Ball received a letter from a man named Robert Partridge, advising that he would be willing to sell the manuscript for three hundred guineas. Partridge wrote that he was in negotiation with an American university about a sale but that he was not very keen on selling it to America. Ball's interest was whetted by Partridge's description of it as "an amazing and unique manuscript which contains a remarkable (unpublished) introduction and foreword by the author." Unable to come up with the asking price from his own resources, Ball did not even reply to the Partridge letter. He had some friends who had promised to contribute ten pounds each to help secure the manuscript, but as Ball later wrote, "when we heard that the price was three hundred guineas, we all agreed to shut up shop."

In August 1946 he received another letter from Partridge saying that he would now agree to sell the manuscript to Ball, and when it came to settling a price, he pointed out that he had received offers of £75 from a dealer. He was aware of Fred's passion for the Tressell story – probably from Grant Richards – and wrote: "I feel some sort of moral responsibility in your having the manuscript – since you have angled for it for so long – but, unfortunately, I am not a charity institution." They finally agreed on a price of £60. Fred quickly consulted the group of friends and they contributed to make up the £60, although Partridge then clarified that it was 60 *guineas* that he meant. In September 1946, Ball and Partridge met at a cafe near the Elephant and Castle underground station in London and the manuscript changed hands there. Later information revealed that when Grant Richards was about to retire he had gifted the manuscript to his long-serving secretary, Pauline Hemmerde, who sold it for £10 when she fell on hard times. Partridge may have been the purchaser.

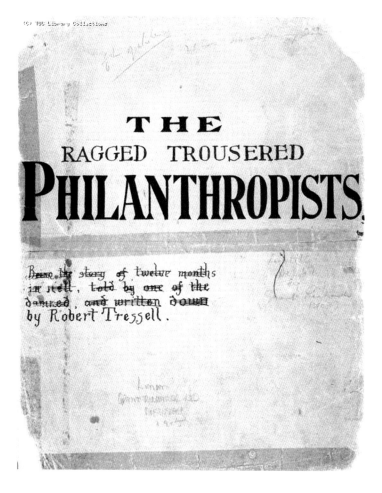

The title page of the manuscript, now in the care of the TUC, and available to read on-line.
(Trades Union Congress Library Collections, London Metropolitan University.)

When the delighted Fred Ball studied the manuscript, he was amazed to discover that the book which was so familiar to him and other readers was considerably shorter than the original manuscript; approximately 100,000 words had been omitted from the 1914 edition and 160,000 words from the 1918 edition. So began Ball's next mission: to have the original manuscript published as its author intended. In the meantime, and for over ten years, he kept the precious manuscript stored under his bed in Hastings.

There were many obstacles to publication, not least the issue of copyright, and where exactly copyright to the unpublished pages lay. But Fred Ball and his wife Jacquie had other practical challenges as well. They found that the original manuscript had been altered in many ways by Jessie Pope. The material published in 1914 had been extracted from the original, and the remainder set aside, breaking Tressell's sequence of pages. The first task was to restore this sequence. Then they had to deal with whole passages which had been changed by Pope, who had literally done a scissors-and-paste job on the original. As Ball described it:

> Some pages were cut through with scissors, a few were missing altogether and the manuscript was liberally sprinkled with the first editor's alterations of the text. Many pages were paraphrased or summarized on separate sheets by Jessie Pope and in some cases she had pasted stiff cards over Tressell's original.

Where possible, Ball removed the pasted papers, but in some cases this was not possible and the original text had to be read from the back. At this time Ball also learned that Pope had altered the author's name to Tressall.

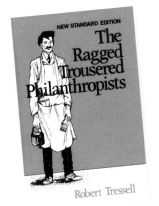

The first complete edition of the novel, 1955. (Steve Peak)

PUBLICATION IN FULL IN 1955

In *Tressell of Mugsborough* Fred Ball included an invitation to readers to come to read Tressell's manuscript on his kitchen table. He was staggered to find that scores of people took up the offer – "writers, students, teachers and workers, including a group of miners from the Scottish pits." This biography stimulated demand for the publication of the original novel in full, and after the copyright issues were eventually overcome, Lawrence and Wishart, publishers of left-wing books, asked Fred Ball to act as editor. *The Ragged Trousered Philanthropists* by Robert Tressell was published in full in October 1955. The print run was 5,000 copies, which included a hardback library edition of 1,500 copies at £1.10 shillings and a 'trade-union' edition of 3,500 which sold at 10 shillings and 6 pence. It sold out completely within three months. Regular reprints followed and it was published in Russia in 1957, in the German Democratic Republic in 1958, and in Czechoslovakia in 1961.

A S HE READ OVER the 1913-14 correspondence between Grant Richards and Jessie Pope in preparation for the publication of the manuscript, Ball came across a letter of August 1913 from Pope in which she wrote: "I have advised Miss Croker to accept your offer." This puzzled him; it clearly referred to Kathleen but why was she called Miss Croker?

The answer was in another letter of November 1913, also from Pope to Grant Richards. Referring to Kathleen, the letter ran as follows:

> She – the nurse – came round to see me yesterday and after requesting a private interview began "I think Miss Pope I had better tell you all about it – my great-grandfather was Sir Samuel Croker." I told her it didn't matter what her great-grandfather was – so long as her father earned his living as a house-painter and really lived among the scenes he described and suffered the privations of an "out-of-work."

Pope went on to say that Kathleen confirmed that he did earn his living as a painter from the age of sixteen to forty-three, "when he died." There are some errors here: Robert did not reach the age of forty-three, and died two months before his forty-first birthday. Ball also notes that Kathleen believed that Croker was her grandfather not great-grandfather, as Pope wrote. Pope's letter went on: "The literary house-painter was really named 'Noonan' or 'Croker' I can't be sure which. His daughter is 'Noonan' but I believe you know her as 'Croker'. I suppose it doesn't matter anyhow."

Ball admits to being put out that neither Grant Richards nor Alice Meiklejon had mentioned the surname Croker earlier in his search. He recalled Alice saying: "I do not at all rule out the possibility that Robert did not take his father's real name. He was very secretive and entirely cut himself off from his family." But she had kept any knowledge of the name Croker to herself.

The authenticity of Robert Tressell's working class credentials was important to his readers, as it had been to his first publishers. Ball records his response to the new information on Sir Samuel Croker: "If anything, although I had doubted his working-class origins since his niece's story, this new disclosure that my famous working-class writer was the son of a gentleman after all, added to my sympathy for his predicament. In particular, it threw a new light on his isolation, his sense of despair and futility which the workers as a class didn't share." Ball also recollected the family information that on the death of his father, "his mother re-married and squandered the family fortune." This was believed to explain why Robert left the family home and left Ireland. But Ball was also was told that Robert was ashamed that his father had made his money from the rents of impoverished tenants in Ireland and rejected the opportunity to study in Trinity College, refusing to live off this unearned income. Instead, he left Ireland, never to return.

No.1 Winslow Terrace, now No.49 Terenure Road East.

Ball decided that he would have to go to Ireland to continue his quest. The publishers Lawrence and Wishart funded a visit by Fred and Jacquie to Dublin where they did some research, gradually piecing together a quite amazing story. His initial discoveries are given here first; they were added to later. They found out that Samuel Croker was a retired policeman who became a Resident Magistrate (RM) and lived at No.1 Winslow Terrace in Rathgar, Dublin. They also found birth certificates for Robert, dated 18th April 1870, and for Adelaide, dated 20th March 1867, to parents Samuel Croker and Mary Croker née Noonan. (Adelaide's birth was on 3rd May 1867, in fact.) The father was described as 'Pensioner' and 'Military Pensioner' respectively.

The Balls' time was limited so they left £3 to cover the cost of a report from the Genealogical Office which was later sent to them. It provided some more surprising details, citing two legal documents and stating that they "would appear to merit careful consideration." One was dated 1873 and showed that Samuel Croker, retired Resident Magistrate of No.1 Winslow Terrace, Rathgar, demised a house on Great Britain Street, Dublin (today's Parnell St.) with an annual rent of £27. 13s. 10d. to Mary Anne Noonan.

The second was a Family Settlement of 1874 which recorded that Samuel Croker, "granted one Mary Noonan an annuity of £100 payable out of his pension." The parties to this second document were named as Samuel, his wife, Jane Usher Croker, and their five children, Annie, Arthur, John, Samuel and Melian. Significantly, Samuel Croker senior is described in this document as "retired Resident Magistrate, of London." The report concluded that, although there was no reference in the documents to a relationship between Samuel and Mary Noonan, "Robert and Adelaide may have been the illegitimate children of Samuel Croker R.M. and Mary Noonan." Finally, the

No.37 Wexford St. today.

report cautiously advised that information on birth certificates is compiled from details supplied by the informant.

Fred Ball accepted that Robert and Adelaide were the illegitimate children of Samuel Croker and Mary Noonan, but he was puzzled at the fact that Mary gave her surname as Croker on birth records. He also acknowledged that he had discovered little about "the identity of Samuel Croker, his professional life and social background." He ended his chapter on the Croker-Noonan lineage of Robert with this sentence: "And there for the time we left it."

Samuel Croker, a married man, had a liaison with Mary Noonan and they had several children. One of these was Robert, born in April 1870, and the record of his baptism in St. Kevin's Church, Dublin confirms this information, with Mary Noonan's address given as No.37 Wexford St. Birth and baptismal records give Robert's surname as Croker, but he later chose to use his mother's surname instead.

Birth details of Robert Croker, born on 18th April 1870. Samuel Croker, pensioner, and Mary Croker, formerly Noonan, are both registered as residing at No.37 Wexford St. (General Register Office, Dublin.)

Birth details of Adelaide Anne Croker, born on 3rd May 1867. Samuel Croker, military pensioner, and Mary Croker, formerly Noonan, are both registered as residing at No.53 Lower Wellington St. (General Register Office, Dublin.)

Jim Herlihy's research on the Royal Irish Constabulary later unearthed more information, such as the various postings of Samuel around Ireland and his address in Dublin in the 1860s. It was clear that he was not knighted and a further remarkable detail emerged: Samuel Croker was born in 1790, so when Robert was born in 1870, his father was aged 80. Mary Noonan must have been about half that age, or even younger.

A return from the dead 5

DRAMATIC REVELATIONS did not end with the discovery of the Croker family background. Because of the great interest in *RTP* and because it had strong dramatic elements, several stage versions had been performed in the years since it was first published. In 1967 the BBC announced that a dramatisation would be broadcast on television. A letter from Reg Johnson appeared in *The Times* pointing out the irony and pathos of the fact that the daughter of the author of *RTP* would be unable to watch the programme as she did not possess a television set. *The Times* then sent a reporter to interview this woman, Kathleen Lynne, and an article appeared on 5th June under the heading: "Sold rights to classic for £25". Kathleen Lynne was indeed the daughter of Robert Noonan, another astonishing revelation, and a bombshell to Fred Ball. Reg Johnson was married to Kathleen's daughter Joan and all three lived together in Winchcombe in Gloucestershire. Fred Ball quickly made arrangements to visit them.

The story of the lives of Robert Noonan's daughter and grand-daughter gradually emerged. Paul Meiklejon and Kathleen were married in July 1914, four days after she arrived in Regina, Saskatchewan. They both worked with a travelling theatre company, where Paul used the stage name Lynne and Kathleen was known as Mrs. Lynne. She enjoyed her adventures touring around the country, appearing at one time in a mind-reading act billed as "Gabrielle Devereaux, the Girl Mystic."

Their daughter Joan was born in November 1915, but all was not well in the marriage and Kathleen attempted to leave Paul several times. She finally left in 1918 and she and Joan settled in Toronto where she continued to use the name Lynne, or sometimes Meiklejon-Lynne. When Paul asked what he would tell their families at home, she replied "Oh, tell them I am dead." He did exactly that, adding that she and Joan had both been killed in a car accident. This story was accepted as fact back in England, at least outside the immediate Meiklejon family circle.

Kathleen became a committed Christian and she once wrote a pamphlet for her church on the slums of Montreal under the title *Hovels for God's Children*. Joan became a novice in an Anglican order of nuns and when she studied in England in the mid-1950s, her mother visited her briefly. When Kathleen

Kathleen Noonan in 1970.
(F. C. Ball, *One of the Damned*)

decided to return permanently to England in 1962, Joan accompanied her. Kathleen died in 1988, at the age of 95.

Alice Meiklejon, who died in 1962, knew all this when she was communicating with Fred Ball and when he was writing his first book, just as she had known about the Croker name, but she chose not to reveal the information to him. Nor did she tell Joan about him and his research. Such was the secrecy around family information that Kathleen believed her mother's name was Madeline until Ball told her it was Elizabeth. Proof that somebody knew of Kathleen's survival was the discovery that Grant Richards had sent her another cheque for £25 in the 1920s. He did not inform Ball of this either.

Back in England in the 1960s, Kathleen had become aware of the popularity of her father's book but was also conscious that she had sold all rights to it. She may have inherited some of her father's dry wit as she told *The Times*: "I don't want to be rich, but I would like to be able to buy some new curtains." She said that she had sold the rights to the book "for a mess of potage" but £25 was a great deal of money to her in 1913 and she understood the risk the publisher was taking. She accepted that it was "a very fair price." She subsequently received some money from the BBC and a gift of a television set and a cheque from Hastings Trades Council. She finally saw the dramatisation of *RTP* when it was re-broadcast in 1969.

Fred Ball met Kathleen frequently, interviewing her about her father and their life together and adding considerably to what was known about their

Joan Johnson and husband Reg.
Joan's death occurred in 2000
and Reg died in 2013.
(Ion Castro, Robert Tressell Society)

time in Hastings. Dave Harker says that her memories were "systematically interrogated" by Ball and that the consistency of her responses was impressive. Kathleen remembered her father as a man "filled with a burning zeal for justice and the betterment of mankind, no matter what the personal cost." She was aware that there were distinctions between what she remembered and what she thought she remembered about her father. While Kathleen's memories from her own childhood can be taken as accurate, her memories of what her father told her about his childhood are less reliable, and her recall of what he actually told her may not be accurate. Her father may well have told fanciful tales to impress a child with a particular heroic image of himself; he was a story-teller, after all, and he is said to have told one man that he was born in Liverpool and another that he was born in London. Fred Ball's reporting of what he heard from Kathleen should also be treated with caution.

Ball had many questions about Robert's parents and early life. Kathleen had a birthday book in which her father wrote under the date 17th April, "Robert Noonan born Dublin, Ireland" although his actual birth-date was 18th April. According to Kathleen, Robert told her he was born in Merrion Square West, and that his father was Sir Samuel Croker, an army officer. She did not know his mother's name, but she was told that she was frivolous, vain and proud of her tiny feet and that she married off her eldest daughter at an early age because she might make her mother look old. Kathleen recalled stories her father told about Samuel, that he was injured in "the Phoenix Park riots," had a silver plate inserted in his skull and that he had died raving as a result of the head injury. Another story was of Samuel capturing a rebel in a remote mountain cabin by tricking him into believing that he was surrounded.

Kathleen said that Robert told her that he spent some of his childhood in London and ran away from the house at one time, dressed in a sailor suit and was found by a policeman sleeping under a tree with a loaf of bread and a carving knife. She also recalled hearing about another childhood incident, when Robert was severely whipped by his father for staying out too long, while his older brother was not punished. Kathleen also believed that Samuel lived in comfort from the rent of estates in Ireland, gave very little attention to his tenants and left the management to agents. In Ball's account, Kathleen believed that Robert, "who was, or was about to become, a student at Trinity College, left home when he decided that he could not live on an income from absentee rentals."

Kathleen had heard nothing from her father about Samuel's death when Robert was a child, or about his mother's re-marriage. As far as she knew, there were three girls and three boys in her father's family. She did not know anything about Robert's education but believed his sisters went to convent schools. Ball's book has no more information about Robert's two brothers, but interestingly he quotes Kathleen as saying that although Robert and his two sisters in Hastings took the name Noonan, "they all thought of themselves as Croker." When discussing the pseudonym he would use for his novel, Robert told her in his sardonic way that he could not use the name Croker, as people would say "Croker by name and croaker by nature". Further information on the Croker/Noonan family background is given in Chapters 9 and 10.

A GRAVE IN LIVERPOOL

Plaque in Liverpool.

Following on the return of Kathleen, there was another closing of the circle with Fred Ball's identification of Robert Noonan's grave in Liverpool in September 1968. Ball had made many attempts to find the grave but was unsuccessful. Then, unexpectedly, he had a positive response from Walton Park cemetery, adjacent to Walton Hospital. He was told that Robert had been buried on 10th February 1911, seven days after his death, in Plot T11, under a Relieving Officer's Order, which meant as a pauper. Fred Ball ended his book with this final discovery, noting the coincidence that nearby was a tombstone to the memory of a family named Owen.

Towards the end of *RTP* there is a reference to the burial of a pauper, who turns out to be Jack Linden, the old man who had worked on "The Cave:"

> It was a very plain-looking closed hearse with only one horse. There was no undertaker in front and no bearers walked by the sides. It was a pauper's funeral. Three men evidently in their Sunday clothes followed behind the

hearse. As they reached the church door, four old men who were dressed in ordinary everyday clothes, came forward and opening the hearse took out the coffin and carried it into the church, followed by the other three, who were evidently relatives of the deceased. The four men were paupers – inmates of the workhouse, who were paid sixpence each for acting as bearers..... The roughly made coffin was of white deal, not painted or covered in any way, and devoid of any fittings or ornaments with the exception of a square piece of zinc on the lid.

Liverpool and Hastings Trades Councils co-operated in raising funds to erect a memorial over Robert Noonan's grave which was unveiled in 1977. In an appropriate tribute, the names of the other twelve paupers (seven of them women) were also recorded on the headstone. A passage from Wolfe Tone was read at the graveside, and Robert's grand-daughter Joan gave a passionate speech, imploring all the factions of the left to unite in solidarity. One trade unionist declared: "They buried Robert Noonan, but they could not bury Robert Tressell." These lines from Chapter 45 of *RTP*, from a poem by William Morris, artist, writer and socialist, are engraved on the memorial:

> *Through squalid lives they laboured*
> *In sordid grief they died*
> *Those sons of a mighty mother,*
> *Those props of England's pride.*
> *They are gone, there is none*
> *Can undo it, nor save our souls*
> *From the curse*
> *But many a million cometh*
> *And shall they be better or worse?*
> *It is we who must answer and hasten*
> *And open wide the door*
> *For the rich man's hurrying terror*
> *And the slow foot hope of the poor.*

These next lines of the poem are not included on the headstone:

> *Yea, the voiceless wrath of the wretched and their unlearned discontent*
> *We must give it voice and wisdom, till the waiting tide be spent.*

Robert Noonan's grave.
(Dee Daly, Robert Tressell
Society)

ROBERT NOONAN'S DIVORCE

In 2001, one more surprising discovery was made by Jonathan Hyslop in the archives in South Africa. It concerned the divorce of Robert and Elizabeth Noonan in 1897. Robert worked in Johannesburg, leaving his wife and daughter in Cape Town for long periods. In April 1896 he went to Cape Town and found her pregnant, and a child was born in August. He had suspicions that the child might not be his, but said nothing and returned to Johannesburg. Elizabeth became ill and he returned to Cape Town and she then told him the child's father was Thomas Lindenbaum, a man to whom her mother introduced her. Elizabeth did not attend to give evidence in the divorce case but Lindenbaum did, saying he had paid her for sex. He also said that she had had a previous affair with a man named Saunders, and Robert confirmed that he knew about that affair, saying he had forgiven her. Nothing is known of Elizabeth's life after the divorce.

Jonathan Hyslop saw the parallels with the Ruth Easton plot in *RTP*. Ruth and William Easton have one child and they are struggling to make ends meet. They take in the despicable Slyme as a lodger, and he ingratiates himself with

Ruth by showing kindness to the little child. As Easton spends more time in the pub, neglecting Ruth's needs, Slyme takes full advantage. When Ruth, who is unused to alcohol, gets drunk on a rare visit to the pub and goes home on her own, Slyme rapes her and she becomes pregnant by him. The child is born but William does not know that the child is not his. Racked by guilt and despair, Ruth makes an attempt to take her own life and that of the child, but circumstances prevent her. Then William learns the truth and is confronted by Owen who tells him:

> "You may not have struck her but you did worse – you treated her with indifference and exposed her to temptation. What has happened is the natural result of your neglect and want of care for her. The responsibility for what happened is mainly yours but apparently you wish to pose now as being very generous and to 'forgive her' – you're willing to take her back; but it seems to me that it would be more fitting that you should ask her to forgive you."

The following day a subdued William accepts the wisdom of the advice and follows it and he and Ruth are reconciled. Frank and Nora Owen agree to take the baby into their family.

Robert Noonan appears to have had no intimate relationships while in Hastings, and he was undoubtedly a lonely man. Jonathan Hyslop's insight into the situation is a perceptive one and he makes the case that William Easton's story reflects aspects of Robert Noonan's life and personality. In an oblique way, the Easton story can be seen as a kind of atonement for him, or as Hyslop expresses it, "an imaginative resolution of the conflicts which Robert Noonan felt about his marriage."

Fred Ball's book, *One of the Damned*, 1979 edition.
(Steve Peak)

6 A novel for our times

IN HIS UNCOMPLETED PREFACE, Robert Tressell declared that his intention was "to present, in the form of an interesting story, a faithful picture of working-class life – more especially of those engaged in the Building trades – in a small town in the south of England." The Preface is likely to have been penned as an apologia to potential publishers. He wrote that he wished to show "the conditions resulting from poverty and unemployment: to expose the futility of the measures taken to deal with them and to indicate what I believe to be the only real remedy, namely – Socialism." He believed that people who opposed socialism did not properly understand it.

He submitted the book to the verdict of readers and continued: "The work possesses at least one merit, that of being true. I have invented nothing. There are no scenes or incidents in the story that I have not either witnessed myself or had conclusive evidence of." He also anticipated objections from readers, some of whom he knew might not like the language in which the characters spoke and he concluded the Preface as follows:

> If the book is published I think it will appeal to a very large number of readers. Because it is true it will probably be denounced as a libel on the working classes and their employers, and upon the religious-professing section of the community. But I believe it will be acknowledged as true by most of those who are compelled to spend their lives amid the surroundings it describes, and it will be evident that no attack is made upon sincere religion.

The story opens with a group of workmen involved in the renovation of a large house in the town of Mugsborough. The opening sentence is: "The house was named 'The Cave.'" There are about twenty-five men involved, working for the firm Rushton and Co. Bob Crass, the painters' foreman, blows his whistle for tea-break. The apprentice Bert White is being teased by Sawkins and Bundy. Frank Owen, who is a socialist and the central character of the book, reads a newspaper as is his custom. "He was generally regarded as a bit of a crank: for it was felt that there must be something wrong about a man who took no interest in racing or football and who was always talking a lot of rot about religion and politics." Another man named Barrington is also quiet and speaks only when spoken to, but he is well liked. Both of these men have some of the attributes and views of Robert Noonan. The other men in the room include:

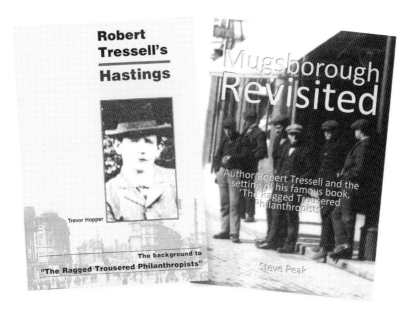

Two books by Hastings local historians, Steve Peak and Trevor Hopper.

Easton, Payne, Harlow, Philpot, Slyme and old Jack Linden. Their rambling exchanges on the quality of the tea, the horses, the Tories "Fissical Policy" and other matters are rendered in their natural speech, with their own slang and colloquialisms. Cross dominates the discussion, declaring "this country is being ruined by foreigners." By way of making his point he says to another man: "You're wot I call a bloody windbag, you've got a 'ell of a lot to say but wen it comes to the point you don't know nothin'."

Owen listens to a range of views on the causes of poverty "with feelings of contempt and wonder. Were they all hopelessly stupid? Had their intelligence never developed beyond the childhood stage? Or was he mad himself?" He becomes involved, sneering at the opinions expressed by the others and he explains what he understands by poverty:

> "What I call poverty is when people are not able to secure for themselves all the benefits of civilisation; the necessaries, comforts, pleasures and refinements of life, leisure, books, theatre, pictures, music, holidays, travel, good and beautiful homes, good clothes, good and pleasant food." Everybody laughed. It was so ridiculous. The idea of the likes of them wanting or having such things! Any doubts that any of them had entertained as to Owen's sanity disappeared. The man was as mad as a March hare.

The foreman, Hunter, is introduced in the second chapter and we learn that he is nicknamed Nimrod and Misery and Pontius Pilate. He is despised, as he can sack men at will: he had the power to deprive them of a living and to deprive their children of bread. He sneaks up on them to try to catch them idling and they are generally in great fear of him.

Owen is married to Nora and they have a son named Frankie. As Owen observes the humiliation of an older man by Misery, he becomes despondent:

> He was more indignant on poor old Linden's account than on his own and was oppressed by a sense of impotence and shameful degradation. All his life it had been the same: incessant work under similar more or less humiliating conditions and with no more result than being just able to avoid starvation.
>
> And the future as far as he could see was as hopeless as the past; darker, for there would surely come a time, if he lived long enough, when he would be unable to work anymore. He thought of his child; was he to be a slave and a drudge all his life also? It would be better for the boy to die now.
>
> As Owen thought of the boy's future there sprung up within him a feeling of hatred and a fury against the majority of his fellow workmen. They were the enemy. Those who not only quietly submitted like so many cattle to the existing state of things, but defended it, and opposed and ridiculed any suggestion to alter it.

Penguin Modern Classic edition.
(Steve Peak)

Later on we meet some of the businessmen of the town, "the Idlers," with names such as Didlum, Grinder and Adam (a damn) Sweater, who is the owner of the house being renovated. Other business firms are named Makehaste and Sloggem, Dauber and Botchit, Smeeriton and Leavit. The two newspapers of Mugsborough are called the *Daily Obscurer* and the *Daily Chloroform*. The members of the Town Council are called The Brigands or The Forty Thieves. Mr. Belcher is a clergyman, Mr. Lettum an estate agent, and Mr. Snatchum an undertaker. Others mentioned are: Mrs. Starvem, Lady Slumrent, Mrs. Knobrane, Mrs. M. T. Head and A. Smallman. Fortunately, not all characters are named for their attributes or occupations in this dated style.

SOCIALISM

In the late 19th century, Toby King was a prominent radical voice in Hastings. He was a giant of twenty-two stone and had a great influence on other radical thinkers. He gave classes on politics and history and took part in campaigns for the vote, for children's rights, and for a free press. King also visited Ireland and wrote a pamphlet with the title *Ireland's Woes and Ireland's Foes*. He died in 1899, before Robert arrived, but his legacy would still have been influential.

Ball says that although there were individual socialists in Hastings at that time, they only began to organise in 1906, the year of the general election.

When Owen is challenged by his fellow workers about what he thinks is the cause of poverty he replies: "The present system – competition – capitalism." Expanding on that, he gives his analysis which has become beloved of radicals everywhere:

> Suppose some people were living in a house.... and suppose they were always ill, and suppose that the house was badly built, the walls so constructed that they drew and retained moisture, the roof broken and leaky, the drains defective, the doors and windows ill-fitting and the rooms badly shaped and draughty. If you were asked to name in a word, the cause of the ill health of the people who lived there you would say – the house. All the tinkering in the world would not make that house fit to live in; the only thing to do with it would be to pull it down and build another. Well, we're all living in a house called the Money System; and as a result most of us are suffering from a disease called poverty. There's so much the matter with the present system that it's no good tinkering at it. Everything about it is wrong and there's nothing about it that's right. There's only one thing to be done with it and that is to smash it up and have a different system altogether. We must get out of it.

He elaborates further:

> Poverty is not caused by men and women getting married; it's not caused by machinery; it's not caused by 'over-production'; it's not caused by 'over-population'. It's caused by Private Monopoly. That is the present system. They have monopolized everything that it is possible to monopolize; they have got the whole earth, the minerals in the earth and the streams that water the earth. The only reason they have not monopolized the daylight and the air is that it is not possible to do it.

Later in the book, Barrington advises that change will be achieved in parliament: "You must fill the House of Commons with Revolutionary Socialists." While the novel is undoubtedly harsh in its depiction of employers and workers alike, the pent-up passion of Robert Tressell for justice and fairness is the core of the book. This is what makes the novel timeless and international and why its appeal is enduring. Robert draws readers into moral questions in Chapter 21 "The Reign of Terror. The Great Money Trick." All the workers cursed Crass, Hunter and Rushton but all would gladly have changed places with them and in those circumstances would have behaved in exactly the same way. The fault was not in individuals, but the System.

> If you, reader, had been one of the hands, would you have slogged? Or would you prefer to starve and see your family starve? If you had been in Crass's

place would you have resigned rather than do such dirty work? If you had had Hunter's berth, would you have given it up and reduced yourself to the level of the hands? If you had been Rushton, would you rather have become bankrupt than treat your 'hands' and your customers in the same way as your competitors treated theirs? It may be that, so placed, you – being the noble-minded paragon that you are – would have behaved unselfishly. But no one has any right to expect you to sacrifice yourself for the benefit of other people who would only call you a fool for your pains.

It may be true that if any one of the hands – Owen, for instance – had been an employer of labour, he would have done the same as other employers. Some people seem to think that proves that the present system is all right! But really it only proves that the present system compels selfishness. One must either trample upon others or be trampled upon oneself. Happiness might be possible if everyone were unselfish; if everyone thought of the welfare of his neighbour before thinking of his own. But as there is only a very small percentage of such unselfish people in the world, the present system has made the earth into a sort of hell..... Blame the system.

Tressell's language in the mouth of Frank Owen is uncompromising and even callous, as when he says that "if people were not so mentally deficient, they would have swept away this silly system." Realising that the elderly Lindens were likely to finish up in the workhouse, Owen is sympathetic, but only to a certain point:

All the same, there's no getting away from the fact that they deserve to suffer. All their lives they've been working like brutes and living in poverty.... All their lives they have supported and defended the system that robbed them, and have resisted and ridiculed every attempt to alter it. It's wrong to feel sorry for such people; they deserve to suffer.

THE GREAT MONEY TRICK

There have been many dramatisations of *RTP* on stage, on television and on radio. One scene in particular is guaranteed to entertain audiences: the Great Money Trick. This is when Owen tries to persuade the men that money is the cause of poverty, a notion at which they guffawed. It is during lunch break and he uses slices of bread from the lunch-boxes, telling them that these are the raw materials. He borrows pocket-knives from three of the men, calling these the machinery of production. Owen represents the capitalist and the three men represent the working class. He tells them not to question how he comes to own the bread and the knives; that is just how it is. Owen also produces three coins to represent his money capital. Each man then cuts up each slice into three little pieces; this represents his work each week. Owen takes the three pieces of bread for himself and gives each man a coin as wages. Owen then explains that the worker must use his coin to buy the necessaries of life from him. The necessaries are represented as one piece of bread which the workers then consume. So Owen, the capitalist, ends up with all the bread piling up beside him and keeps getting back the money he pays in wages, while the workers have nothing. This pattern continues for some time until Owen suddenly decides to shut everything down because, due to over-production, there is a glut on the market. The workers are dismissed with nothing to show for all their work. When they ask what they are meant to do, this is what they are told:

"That's not my business," replied the kind-hearted capitalist, "I've paid you your wages and provided you with Plenty of Work for a long time past. I have no more work for you to do at present. Come round again in a few months time and I'll see what I can do for you."

When they ask how they are to buy the necessaries of life, the capitalist says: "You should have been more thrifty. Look how I have got on by being thrifty!" The demonstration ends with the workers becoming truculent and the capitalist threatening that "he would have their faces battered in for them by the police." Although Karl Marx does not get a mention in *RTP*, Tressell's exposition of the Great Money Trick is regarded as an entertaining and graphic presentation of a core Marxist principle, the labour theory of value.

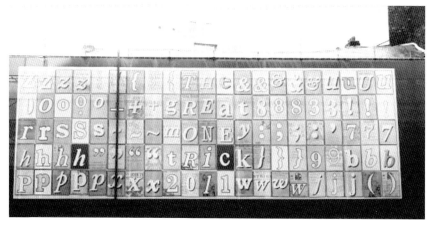

The Great Money Trick – a display in Liverpool during the City of Radicals celebrations of 2011.

THE FORTY THIEVES

Each generation of readers can find something of relevance in *RTP* and the shenanigans of the businessmen of Mugsborough have a resonance for aggrieved Irish citizens today. The business men are collectively called The Idlers and they are also the members of the Municipal Council, called The Brigands and The Forty Thieves. The blinkered public of Mugsborough elect these men because "the fact that a man had succeeded in accumulating money in business was a clear demonstration of his fitness to be entrusted with the business of the town." In office, they do as they please and never consult the ratepayers, and yet they are always re-elected. In a metaphor for all the ways in which public officials can take advantage of their position, the councillors purloin the best plants from the public parks for their own gardens, and when the geese and ducks are nicely fattened in the park lakes, they bring them home to eat, and when they are sated, they sell the remainder to butchers.

When they enviously observe the success of the Gas Company, these avaricious men of substance decide to buy a vacant site from the Council, of which they are the chief members, at a knockdown price. They set up an electricity company and when it flounders on the brink of bankruptcy, they adopt a scheme to inflate the share price and use the press to convince the public that the company is very successful. At this point the businessmen sell it back to the Council for much more than it is actually worth. The one councillor who found this and other sharp practices objectionable is called Dr. Weakling and he is well-meaning but isolated and ineffective against the majority – like some latter-day regulators. At the end, the businessmen congratulate themselves on their successful scam and drink a toast to public ownership, deciding that it will prove a double victory for them, as "when the ratepayers 'ave bought the Works, and they begins to kick up a row because they're losin' money over it – we can tell 'em that it's Socialism! And then they'll say that if that's Socialism they don't want no more of it!"

Irish readers would identify with the scorn and outrage of Robert Tressell at the excesses of the Idlers and the Forty Thieves. In recent years an astonishing number of financial scandals have come to light during, and in the wake of, the years of the "Celtic tiger." "Golden circles" and "bailouts" were the stuff of daily news for several years, with the state using taxpayers' money to rescue bankers, speculators and developers. These scandals followed on a succession of cases of political and planning corruption when "brown envelopes" and backhanders were common.

The discussions in the Mugsborough Council boardroom have uncanny echoes of the exchanges between executives of a prominent bank, as recorded on tape and released to the Irish media in 2013. The kind of boardroom chicanery and arrogance revealed in Mugsborough Council was also heard among the buccaneering executives of the bank, where macho officials sneeringly celebrated news of EU rescue funds by singing "Deutschland Über Alles" and saying they would "stick the fingers up" to the regulator's concerns. Referring to Irish government financial aid, one official said: "The strategy here is you pull them in, you get them to write a big cheque and then they have to support their money." When transcripts of these tapes were circulated in 2013, the public was outraged, and one journalist in Tressellian indignation described the behaviour as "arrogant, cynical, greedy, contemptuous, myopic and feckless."

Recent controversies about lavish pensions paid to retired politicians and public servants, and top-up payments to executives, have left the Irish public incandescent with rage at the sense of self-entitlement that exists in the board-rooms of corporations. At a time of extreme cuts to vital welfare and health services, revelations that public money, and even money donated to charity, was used to provide extravagant salaries and pensions for executives have generated deep resentment. These controversies have many echoes in *RTP*. For example, when the wealthy MP, Sir Graball D'Encloseland, was promoted to a higher office "in the country that he owned such a large part of, he was not only to have a higher and more honourable position, but also – as was nothing but right – a higher salary. His pay was to be increased to seven thousand five hundred a year or one hundred and fifty pounds per week."

RELIGION

Robert Tressell was aware that his novel would shock and outrage many readers and the last line of his Preface reads: "It will be evident that no attack is made upon sincere religion." He was an admirer of "the lowly Carpenter of Nazareth – the Man of Sorrows, who had not where to lay his head," but as the following extracts show, Robert was affronted by the hypocrisy and cant of some of those who called themselves Christians:

> Although none of these self-styled 'Followers' of Christ ever did the things that Jesus said, they talked a great deal about them...... They stigmatized as infidels all those who differed from them, forgetting that the only real infidels are those who are systematically false and unfaithful to the Master they pretend to love and serve.

And again:

> It was not necessary to call in the evidence of science, or to refer to the supposed inconsistencies, impossibilities, contradictions and absurdities contained in the Bible, in order to prove that that there was no truth in the Christian religion. All that was necessary was to look at the conduct of the individuals who were its votaries.

Frank Owen is an atheist and this is a source of interest to the other men and their families. When Owen visited Linden's house, old Mrs. Linden, a religious woman, "looked curiously at the Atheist as he entered the room. He had taken off his hat and she was surprised to find that he was not repulsive to look at, rather the contrary."

Nora and Frank Owen deal with some of their son's questions about religion. Nora tells him that of all those who live without doing any necessary work, the vicar was the very worst. She explains:

"Well, the vicar goes about telling the Idlers that it's quite right for them to do nothing, and that God meant them to have nearly everything that is made by those who work. In fact he tells them that God made the poor for the use of the rich. Then he goes to the workers and tells them that God meant them to work very hard and to give all the good things they make to those who do nothing, and that they should be very thankful to God and to the Idlers for being allowed to have even the very worst food to eat and the rags, and broken boots to wear."

Robert Noonan was an atheist, yet Kathleen said that he lived the most Christian life she had ever come in contact with. He had little time for organised religion and is quoted as saying: "There is only one religion as ridiculous as the Roman Catholic and that is the Protestant." He certainly knew the bible and there are many direct references to it: for example, one church is called "The Church of the Whited Sepulchre," in a clear echo of the scene in the temple where the money changers are scattered by Jesus. Robert also describes Mugsborough in the same Biblical terms: its "fair outward appearance was deceitful. The town was really a vast whited sepulchre." When he is in a fury of denunciation and excoriation, Robert can resemble a Jeremiah threatening terrible retribution. In Marion Walls' analysis of philosophical and religious aspects of the novel she points out the irony of the fact that *RTP* itself has often been described as "the painters' bible" or "the workers' bible." In one description of what socialism means, Tressell is explicitly biblical in his language: "Socialism means peace on earth and goodwill to all mankind."

HUMOUR

There is no doubt that the novel is a crusading and didactic work, but it is not a tract or a treatise. Robert wrote in the Preface: "My main object was to write a readable story full of human interest and based on the happenings of everyday life, the subject of Socialism being treated incidentally." There are many moments of earthy humour and in the many dramatic adaptations these have provided rich entertainment; music and song are very significant throughout the novel also.

Much of the humour comes from the dialogue and repartee among the men and it is hard to convey out of context. One example is when Owen is showing them the Great Money Trick, he produces three halfpenny coins but says that it would be better if he had three sovereigns. Philpot retorts: "I'd lend you some, but I left me purse on our grand pianner." There is earthy humour on "the art of flatulence," a good deal of irony and sarcasm and many puns.

One of the most amusing episodes is the "however trifling" incident. When a worker gathers up rotten wood from old floorboards for use as firewood at home, Misery "kicked up a devil of a row" and threatened to sack on the spot anyone found taking anything away from the site. When they collected their wages at the end of the week, each worker received a printed card from the employer, Rushton, declaring: "Under no circumstances is any article or material, however trifling, to be taken away by workmen for their private use, whether waste material or not.... Any man breaking this rule will be either dismissed without notice or given into custody."

Some men openly defy their employer by tearing up the card in full view of Rushton and Misery, and one throws it into Rushton's face with an obscene curse, and walks off the job. Word spreads around among other workers in the town and they jibe at Rushton's employees calling out "However trifling!" or "Look out chaps! 'Ere comes some of Rushton's pickpockets!" The men working for Rushton begin to use the term "however trifling" as a greeting and a standing joke among themselves. If one of them was spotted going home with a lot of paint or whitewash on his overalls, he would be cautioned by the others about stealing materials. One man makes up a mock list of rules, which includes the weighing of each man in the morning and again as he left in the evening, to ensure that he was not taking any materials home with him. Finally, Tressell has an incident in which Rushton reads his post at breakfast one morning, and on opening one envelope, finds that it contains a copy of one of his own notices – smeared in human excrement. This is one of several ways in which the workers get their own back with small victories over employers, an aspect of the book which continues to appeal to workers with grievances against foremen and employers.

The opening sentences of Chapter 20, entitled "The Forty Thieves. The Battle: Brigands versus Bandits," are disarmingly and charmingly honest. At a stage in the book when readers might well be flagging, Robert seems to be well aware of how much he is demanding of them. He addresses readers directly: "This is an even more usually dull and uninteresting chapter, and introduces several matters that may appear to have nothing to do with the case. The reader is nevertheless entreated to peruse it, because it contains certain information necessary to an understanding of this history."

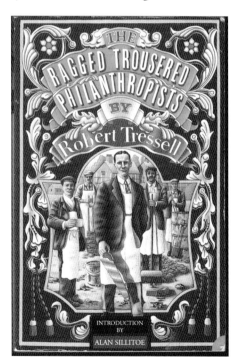

Harper Perennial edition.

DESTITUTION

Some of the most moving scenes in the novel are those describing the utter destitution of the labouring class when winter digs deep and workers are laid off. Men walk about aimlessly, sometimes begging from the public, while the well-to-do complain of the nuisance they caused. In February, three men die of destitution on the streets, while unemployment and the workhouse are spectres that haunt whole families.

Robert had no time for church charity or for benevolent societies as a solution to these problems of the poor, as they degraded people and covered over the real issues:

> These 'charitable' people went into the wretched homes of the poor and – in effect – said: 'Abandon every particle of self-respect: cringe and fawn: come to church: bow down and grovel to us and in return we'll give you a ticket that you can take to a certain shop and exchange for a shillingsworth of groceries. And, if you are very servile and humble, we may give you another one next week.....
>
> Although the people who got the grocery and coal orders, the 'Nourishment', and the cast-off clothes and boots, were very glad to have them, yet these things did far more harm than good. They humiliated, degraded and pauperized those who received them, and the existence of the societies prevented the problem being grappled with in a sane and practical manner.

The situations endured by workers include "petty tyrannies, insults and indignities" inflicted on them by unsympathetic employers and foremen. But they also include the more serious injustices of unsafe working conditions, arbitrary lay-offs and dismissals, inadequate pay and long periods of unemployment.

Nowadays, the situations described by Tressell in the book are regarded as historical in the wealthy north, but in the third world, similar conditions are endured by many workers, in the clothing sweatshops of Bangladesh, for example. Cairnie and Walls claim that a type of Great Money Trick is being played by the corporations and financiers of the global north against the poor south, and that migrant workers also can often be victims of gross exploitation. Tressell was making the case for fair trade, a fair wage for a fair day's work, for equity, for proper safety standards and for a share in profits. This explains why his book remains so relevant and why new editions continue to be published in English, with translations in Bulgaria (1964), Japan (1971), France (1973), Russia (1987), Germany (2002), and Turkey (2006) among other countries.

DESPAIR AND HOPE

One narrative thread of the novel is Frank Owen's deep concern for the future of his wife Nora and his son, Frankie. Early in the book he reads an account in a local newspaper of a man who killed his wife and two children and then took his own life. This was based on an actual press report of 1905, and it is a tragically familiar type of news story today. In *RTP*, the father was driven to this course of action by extreme poverty and despair, and he leaves a note saying "This is not *my* crime but society's." Owen reads in the newspaper that the incident was believed to have occurred "during a fit of temporary insanity brought on by the sufferings the man had endured." His response is:

> "Insanity!" muttered Owen, as he read this glib theory. "Insanity! It seems to me that he would have been insane if he had *not* killed them." Surely it was wiser and better and kinder to send them all to sleep, than to let them continue to suffer.

At various points in the book Owen is "gradually abandoning himself to hopelessness" and considers whether he and his wife and son might be better off dead, especially when he begins to cough up blood and realises that his tuberculosis will overcome him, an experience that is drawn from Robert Noonan's own life. Owen's conclusion is: "If he could not stay with them, they would have to come with him. It would be kinder and more merciful."

Even towards the end of the book his anxieties continue to plague him: "Although he was often seized with a kind of terror of the future – of being unable to work – he fought against these feelings and tried to believe that when the weather became warmer he would be all right once more." This struggle to maintain his spirits is a conflict for him, and when he later speaks optimistically to Nora, he is "affecting a cheerfulness which he did not feel."

By this time, they have willingly adopted the unwanted child of Ruth Easton, and Owen assures Nora that they would easily accommodate an extra member of the family. This little child brings solace and hope:

> As he spoke, he leaned over and touched the head of the sleeping child and the little fingers closed round one of his with a clutch that sent a thrill through him. As he looked at this little helpless, dependent creature, he realised with a kind of thankfulness that he would never have the heart to carry out the dreadful project he had sometimes entertained in hours of despondency. "We've always got through somehow or other," he repeated, "and we'll do so still."

In spite of this revival of his personal spirits, Owen has a vision of tumultuous events to come for mankind:

> In every country, myriads of armed men waiting for their masters to give them the signal to fall upon and rend each other like wild beasts. All around was a state of dreadful anarchy; abundant riches, luxury, vice, hypocrisy, starvation and crime. Men literally fighting with each other for the privilege

of working for their bread, and little children crying with hunger and cold and slowly perishing of want.

However, the note of personal hope in spite of adversity is echoed on the final page of the novel when Owen has a vision of the nemesis of the Capitalist System, and in its crumbling ruins he detects "the glorious fabric of the Cooperative Commonwealth." This is the reason why many readers see the novel as ultimately about hope. The concluding apocalyptic lines of the book are:

> Mankind, awaking from the long night of bondage and mourning and arising from the dust wherein they had lain prone so long, were at last looking upward to the light that was riving asunder and dissolving the dark clouds which had so long concealed from them the face of heaven. The light that will shine upon the world wide Fatherland and illumine the gilded domes and glittering pinnacles of the beautiful cities of the future, where men shall dwell together in true brotherhood and good will and joy. The Golden Light that will be diffused throughout all the happy world from the rays of the risen sun of Socialism.

For Dave Harker, the novel is ultimately about hope, "about socialist values and their continued relevance when we are being told that capitalism is here forever; that greed is good; that war, famine, poverty and racism and every form of oppression are natural, normal and permanent features of life on Planet Earth."

MANY PUBLIC FIGURES in British left-wing and trade union circles became fervent admirers of *RTP*, notwithstanding its shortcomings as a novel. It has influenced generations of socialists and Tony Benn saw it as "a torch to be passed from generation to generation." Michael Foot described it as "the bible of trade union organisers and working class agitators" and regarded it as "a misshapen masterpiece." George Orwell described *RTP* as "a wonderful book, although very clumsily written." There have been criticisms of Tressell's style and technique as a writer, but the academic Raymond Williams wrote this tribute to his gift for dialogue: "There is no finer representation anywhere in English writing of a certain rough-edged mocking, give-and-take conversation between working-men and mates. This humour, this edge, is one of the most remarkable achievements." It is extraordinary that a man who lived in England for such a relatively short period could take on the challenge of conveying the rhythms of the colloquial speech and language of the workers of his adopted town and succeed so well.

The novelist Alan Sillitoe, who came from a working-class family in Nottingham, told of how the book was handed to him in Malaya when he was in the army. He was told: "You ought to read this. Among other things it is the book which won the '45 election for Labour." He saw it as "the first good English novel about the class war" and he said that he was "haunted" by it ever after his first reading. In the introduction to the 1964 edition, he wrote:

> Those whose life has touched the misery recounted by Robert Tressell can get out of it many things: a bolstering of class feeling; pure rage; reinforcement for their own self-pity; a call to action; maybe a good and beneficial dose of all these things.

Dave Harker's book *Tressell* has many tributes from public figures. Jack Beeching is one who is quoted: "Go into any waiting room of the working class movement in Britain and you will find at least one man present who could say 'That book brought me into the movement. That book made me a convinced socialist. That book altered the whole course and direction of my life.'" For another man, "the final message is that the world hasn't got to be like this, it can be changed and life can be good if we fight to make it so." George Hicks, President of the Trades Union Congress (TUC) saw Tressell as "the Zola of building trade operatives.... What he has described is true to life; we know that he lived it."

Jonathan Hyslop has summarised the book's influence as follows:

> No book shaped the 20th century British Labour movement as powerfully as Robert Tressell's *RTP*. In the 70 years from its first posthumous publication amidst the syndicalist fervour of 1914 to the defeat of industrial unionism in the miners' strike of 1984, *RTP* was the left's semi-underground classic, its copies passed by hand from one activist to another and hence from one political generation to another.

By contrast Mervyn Jones, a former Communist, wrote an assessment of *RTP* which might be shared by some readers: "The description of the book as a classic is, in my opinion, great nonsense. What Tressell did was to set down what he heard and saw with great honesty and in laborious imitation of the worst and most cliché-ridden prose of his age. And to set it *all* down." He found it stilted, disliked its "long expositions of socialism" and believed that Owen was "such an insufferable prig that it's no wonder that he converted nobody." He also found the ending "phony, contrived and unworthy." Nevertheless, Jones accepted that the book was "the most detailed, fact-stored, utterly authentic account of working class life and labour that we possess."

Barbara Salter, who did an MA thesis on the novel in 1971, described the book as "nearly great" but she too was sharply aware of its faults:

> Stark reality and absurd fantasy, vivid comedy and laboured propaganda are brought together in this novel, where neither plot nor character analysis predominate. There is much repetition, poor structuring, tired prose. The arguments are rarely intellectually exciting, nor are they fully wedded to the narrative. The end is contrived.

John Monks was TUC General Secretary from 1993 to 2003. He read *RTP* as a teenager in Manchester and he captures the essence of the appeal of the book to many readers like him:

> It is one man's cry against injustice, but it is a solitary cry which has strengthened the resolve of many, myself included, to do what we can to change the world for the better and root out the modern equivalents of the inequality against which he rages so eloquently.

Actor Ricky Tomlinson was advised to read *RTP* by the prison governor while he served a sentence in solitary confinement. Tomlinson says the book changed his life and he believes that its message is still relevant.

> It's the most important book I've ever read in my life. Not only did it change my life politically, it stirred up again in me the beauty of reading.... At times it would make you weep.

A celebration of Robert Tressell in Hastings. Actor Ricky Tomlinson is holding the mug.
John Nettleton, far left, was a great champion of the author in Liverpool. John passed
away in 2007.
(Robert Tressell Society).

Roy Hattersley, writing in the *New Statesman* of 7th February 2011 to mark
the centenary of Robert Noonan's death, gave a harsh but perceptive assessment
of the novel. "Judged purely as a work of fiction, it lacks all distinction and its
arguments – although driven home with a repetitive intensity which was meant
to make new converts – are so crudely simplistic that they are likely to appeal
only to readers who share the author's belief before they open the book."
Hattersley, who was Deputy Leader of the Labour Party from 1983 to 1992,
described it as "the bible of sentimental socialists" and refers to its "depressing
spirit:" He concluded:

> The importance of *The Ragged Trousered Philanthropists* is the emphasis it
> places on the need to change the whole social system. Its weakness is its
> assumption that the working class is too craven and corrupt to work
> gradually to achieving that end.

In *The Guardian* in 2011, Tony Benn, a lifelong admirer of *RTP*, wrote that he
had given the book to many, many people over many years, and all the
recipients had been as inspired by it as much as he had been. His son, Hilary
Benn MP, is also an admirer. Tony marked the centenary of Robert's death by
arguing that his ideas were still important:

> Robert Tressell, through the voice of Frank Owen, is addressing us with
> arguments that are just as relevant now as they were when he first used them

a century ago. If we want to make progress we have to do it ourselves and believe it can be done. That is why this book should be read and studied by this generation if we are to make progress, for there is no other way. We do it ourselves or it will never be done.

The verdict of Michael Foot, former leader of the Labour Party, captures the force of the novel, and the reason for its enduring appeal:

> Some books seem to batter their way to immortality against all the odds, by sheer brute artistic strength, and high up in this curious and honourable company must be counted *The Ragged Trousered Philanthropists*. Robert Tressell's unfailing humour mixes with an unfailing rage and the two together make a truly Swiftian impact.

Today, the achievement of Robert Tressell is honoured in the town where he lived and where he wrote. Hastings Museum and Art Gallery has examples of his art work and local historians have published books and guides to where he lived and to the various locations mentioned in the novel. The houses where he lived are marked with plaques. The Robert Tressell Society is based in Hastings and it has hosted many commemorative events over the years, including academic seminars and workshops. The proceedings have been published. Following the death of Reg Johnson in 2013, the Robert Tressell Family Papers are now in the course of being catalogued in the archives of the University of Brighton at Hastings.

Plaque at No.1 Plynlimmon Road, Hastings

Liverpool has also honoured Robert Tressell in recent years, especially during its commemoration of the centenary of the Great Strike which took place in the city a few months after Robert's death. This "City of Radicals" commemoration in 2011 included a large mural depicting the Great Money Trick and a re-enactment of his funeral. There were plays, unveilings of plaques and laying of wreaths as part of the city's formal tributes to him.

In Dublin, Robert Tressell was remembered in 1991 when a plaque was unveiled at No.37 Wexford St. Joan Johnson and a delegation from Hastings attended the event, the first occasion when his Irish roots were acknowledged. More recently, a plaque in his honour was unveiled by Ruairi Quinn, T.D., the current Minister of Education, at Dublin Writers Museum on Parnell Square in 2002.

In 1996, Waterstones and Channel 4 conducted a poll to find the 100 most influential novels of the 20th century and *RTP* was ranked number 62. In a survey of MPs in 1997, *RTP* was joint winner of the title best political book; the other was Machiavelli's *The Prince*. When *RTP* was broadcast as the classic serial on BBC Radio 4 in 2008, the *Radio Times* promotion went as follows:

Pictured at the unveiling of the plaque at No.37 Wexford St. in May, 1991. From left: Paddy Coughlan, chairman of Dublin Trades Council, Peter Cassells, general secretary of Irish Congress of Trade Unions and Joan Johnson, grand-daughter of Robert Noonan.
(Reg Johnson)

"Fat cat bosses cream off the profits while their workers accept longer hours for less pay in order to keep their jobs. There's a modern resonance here." Playwright Howard Brenton adapted the story for theatre in 2011 and marvelled at how the Great Money Trick never failed to work "for the angry, sharp and sympathetic audience" in Liverpool and "for the more conservative, though equally alert audience" in Chichester. (*The Guardian*, 5th February, 2011.)

A survey of readers' comments on-line today shows that Tressell has lost none of his power to move, to inspire, to convert, to infuriate. There are many reader responses on the guestbook section of the website of the Robert Tressell Society, www.1066.net/tressell. The following extracts are found on the website www.goodreads.com.

- It is rightly heralded as a classic piece of working-class literature, as it takes you into the brutish yet everyday horrors endured by the British working-class, at a time when socialism was beginning to gain ground. One of the most arresting aspects is how little our lives have changed in the time since it was written....

- There are no shades of grey in this novel, and the author believes that if you have a point to make, don't make it once when you can do it twenty times. Additionally the solution presented in the book with the benefit of being able to look back at the 20th century is naive to say the least. What however endures in this book beyond any doubt and provides it with a compelling voice even today is what happens when the weak have no rights, the inhumanity of greed, and finally the self defeating cooperation the oppressed show the oppressors....

- I have always been a bookworm and can say hand on heart that this is one

Robert Tressell is remembered in Dublin Writers Museum, Parnell Square.

of two books that I call the best books I have ever read. The other is *To Kill a Mockingbird*. I cannot explain to people why I love this book as much as I do, it is the only book that has ever made me laugh and cry....

- This biting and bitter social satire was declined by publishers in Robert Tressell's lifetime which says much about the prevailing social order that the novel criticises, for it is as uncomfortable for the establishment as it is powerful for the reader. It is now a century since it was written but the book (sometimes called the bible of socialism, sometimes the first working class novel) remains as broadly relevant today as it did in the period just before the First World War....

- Tressell conveys a message about human needs and requirements and uses Socialism as a tool to point out the flaws of the current system of living, and how we may emerge into a more balanced social order, for all peoples....

- What a book! This is a novel exposing greed, corruption and the pusillanimous nature of the class system which is as relevant today as it was on the day it was published....

- Just an incredible, incredible book. I started off reading it as a Conservative, and by the time I had finished I had decided I would probably join the union at work, and consider voting Labour at the next election! I hadn't heard of it before, but have since discovered how influential this book was at the time of publication, and it is very easy to see why....

• It may not be a great literary work, but it is a book with something to say, and that something is worth taking time to listen to. I think it is fair to say that Tressell has not much more than a rudimentary knowledge of economics, and many of the characters are little more than caricatures or ciphers. The satire is sometimes heavy handed, but the tone of cynicism belies the impression that the author retains some spark of hope, and faith in humanity, that the working man will one day rise up and alleviate his miserable condition....

• Satire, social commentary, socialist tract: this book is all three. The poverty of the craftsmen at its heart – and also their humanity – is especially well-done. The seeds of much that afflicts us now are all too apparent....

• A marvellous book – I would wonder why I had never heard of or read it, were the answer not so glaringly obvious. An unabashed, unapologetic defence of both socialism and atheism, deeply critical of capitalism and Christianity to an extent that could be called harsh if it were not so painfully true; all the more worthwhile given that we seem to be on the path to return to the social and economic conditions of the late nineteenth century....

• One of the best books I have ever read, and that's from a lifelong Tory. It brings home why there was a need for social reform, and indeed the formation of trade unions.... A wonderful, thought-provoking read....

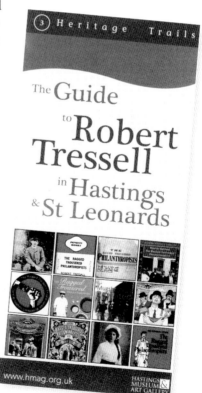

A Heritage Trail by Hastings Museum and Art Gallery.
(Steve Peak)

8 Irish echoes

THE STARK FACT about the first twenty years of Robert Noonan's life is that, up to now, very little has been known for certain. His birth in Dublin in 1870 was recorded, as was his marriage in Cape Town in 1891, but nothing else had been discovered about the years in between. There was no certainty about how long he spent in Ireland. Charles Callan pointed this out in an essay in *Saothar, The Journal of the Irish Labour History Society* in 1997: "However, it must be emphasised that there is no evidence that Noonan either spent his childhood or youth in Ireland." Some biographers, I believe, have drawn unwarranted conclusions from, and given too much credence to, the family stories about Robert's childhood in Ireland.

In a recent academic analysis of *RTP*, Marion Walls discusses the impact of Robert's Irish roots on *RTP*. In a review of what was known of Robert's childhood background, and the wider spectrum of Irish history, she wrote:

> On the paternal side, then, Tressell was heir to instances of religious intolerance, colonial conquest, the land question, and racial politics – in short the history of the oppressor in Ireland. In contrast he was brought up by a mother who was native Irish, Catholic, and as such, one of a marginalised and colonised group. Moreover, being illegitimate, Tressell is not the legitimate heir of either side of the divide. Not surprisingly, then, Tressell grew up with a fragmented and alienated identity, which was further aggravated in South Africa.

Certainly, Robert's childhood could be called fragmented and this must have had a considerable impact on his adult life, although making him heir to the full panoply of complexities of Ireland's history is overstating the case. Hyslop also notes the colonial aspects of his life, saying that as an outsider in Hastings he had a unique perspective, coming from the near colonial world of Ireland and the far colonial world of Africa, and that he observed the lives of the workers of Hastings with a starkness that an English writer could not have.

I set out to find more information on the first half of Robert's life, the years 1870 to 1891, and many significant new facts have been discovered about his early years. More information about the lives of his parents, his siblings and his half-siblings has also been found, and all this will be discussed in Chapter 10.

The questions I began with were: How long did he spend in Ireland? Where in Ireland did he live? Where was he educated? What was the nature of his relationship with his parents? How much did he know about the family situation of his father and his other family? Was he really planning to attend Trinity College? Why did he lose contact with Ireland? Why and how did he go to South Africa? Why does Ireland feature so little in *RTP*? Where did Robert learn his trade? How important to him was the nationalist spirit which he showed in South Africa? How close was he to MacBride and Griffith? Was he aware of the mobilisation of the workers by the charismatic Jim Larkin in Belfast in 1907 and in Dublin after that? Why is so little known about his first twenty years?

The information which we have about Robert's early years comes from his daughter Kathleen, who passed on to Fred Ball what she remembered of what her father had told her about his early life. This happened when she was in her mid-seventies and far removed from her childhood memories. While Kathleen's memory of her father in South Africa and in Hastings was highly significant and wonderful to have recorded, her impressions of his life in Ireland are less reliable, coming as they must have from his accounts, which might have been fanciful tales, partially recalled by her. Some information which Robert imparted about his father was not accurate: he was not "Sir" Samuel Croker, and he did not live in Merrion Square. In this light, many of the other details which Kathleen remembered in old age could also have been inaccurate.

Fred Ball also obtained family information from Robert's niece Alice Meiklejon, daughter of Mary Jane. Early in his quest, Ball was told by Alice that she knew very little about Robert's parentage and background "as this subject was hardly ever referred to by my mother, his sister." In a significant remark, Alice said that "the whole subject of the family history was taboo in the later life of the sons and daughters."

Alice told Fred Ball that Robert was not a working-class man in origin, and that she believed that his father was a well-educated Irishman of Dublin. She understood that he was a very happy child, very sensitive and very fond of his father. Kathleen believed that Robert had a very happy and secure upbringing, in a Catholic environment, with a good education. According to Fred Ball, Kathleen recalled that Robert could speak about seven languages and she listed "Gaelic" as one of them. It is possible that he impressed her as a child with phrases which made him seem more fluent than he was. It would be very unusual if he actually had a fluency in spoken Irish at that time.

Alice believed that after the death of Samuel, Mary Noonan married "again" but rather too soon for Robert's liking. He did not get on with the new man in the household and therefore decided to leave home at sixteen. Kathleen's story was that Robert was offered the opportunity to go to Trinity College, but refused on principle because he believed that his father's money was earned on the backs of poor tenants and he did not wish to benefit from this injustice. Whatever the circumstances, Robert became independent in early life, reaching South Africa by the age of twenty; he would later meet up with some of his sisters in England but there is no evidence of him meeting his mother or other siblings again.

Kathleen recalled little snippets of her father's Irish interests: he sang Irish melodies, and he read authors such as Jonathan Swift and Bram Stoker. He had "the greatest admiration for Swift" and clearly his satirical depictions of hypocrisy and sham stem from the same "savage indignation" (*saeva indignatio*) of Swift. The Latin phrase comes from Swift's epitaph, which he wrote himself.

But Robert seems to have told her nothing of any significance about his mother or siblings. He was described as extremely reticent. Some of the family memories recounted in Fred Ball's book smack of stories told by a father to a child in play. When Kathleen recalled telling Jessie Pope about Sir Samuel Croker, she told Ball that Pope probably thought she was "romancing." The word might be a good term for the kind of stories which a father would tell to an impressionable child in play; maybe Robert was "romancing" about his early life. The story about his father being injured in the Phoenix Park riots is one which does not stand up to scrutiny. The only Phoenix Park riots which I can trace took place in the summer of 1871, long after Samuel Croker had retired from the Constabulary. The incident referred to a confrontation between the police and a group of people demonstrating for an amnesty for Fenian prisoners. Samuel, aged 81, was retired at that time, and it is highly unlikely that he would have been among the demonstrators who were injured when the police baton charged the crowd.

The issue of Robert's refusal to attend Trinity College may be more "romancing" or a fanciful tale. Trinity was an exclusive institution in Irish society, with its students coming from schools and families regarded as elite. Whether Robert was religious or not in his youth, he was nominally a Catholic at least, and it would have been difficult for him to enter Trinity College or to fit in there. Jonathan Hyslop states that the "rebellion" by which Robert refused to go to Trinity because the privilege would be due to "the rents derived from the impoverished Irish peasantry" was a highly significant decision: "This was a pivotal point in Robert's life because this nationalist identification decided his higher education and forced him into life as a manual labourer." But the evidence to support the story is too slender to accept it as a fact, and by the time Robert was ready for university his father was long dead, so the notion of a rebellion against his dead father because of the source of his wealth is implausible.

Robert may have left Ireland when he left home; Kathleen thought that he left Liverpool for South Africa around 1888, at age eighteen, working his passage on board ship. Alice and Kathleen thought that he might not have served an actual apprenticeship and that he probably acquired his skills in South Africa. Charles Callan has done a thorough study of trade union records in Dublin and has found no trace of Robert doing an apprenticeship there. It is possible that he never did a formal apprenticeship.

On one occasion in the workplace Robert heard himself called "a bloody Irishman." Fred Ball wrote that people noticed a slight Irish accent in Robert's speech but Kathleen did not agree. She did recall him singing Irish airs such as "My Dark Rosaleen", "Come Back to Erin" and "The Harp That Once" – popular songs of Thomas Moore. He had an Italian harp with only five strings on it and he played Irish jigs. He admired Wolfe Tone and Robert Emmett, and Kathleen recalls him saying that Ireland would not have Home Rule until it "got rid of the priests and the whiskey."

Kathleen remembered that a Fr. George O'Callaghan was a regular caller to their house in Hastings and the two men used to stay up late at night talking. I have found some biographical information on Fr. O'Callaghan in the archives of the Pallotine order of priests. Despite his name, he was not Irish-born but was from Nova Scotia. He was three years younger than Robert, and was ordained in 1901. He was stationed in Star of the Sea parish in Hastings up to 1910, when he was sent to Florence; in 1912 he was sent to New York where he died in 1928. This revealing note is in the Pallotine archives:

> There is an oral tradition that a Fr. O'Callaghan, stationed in Hastings, was very kind to the Irish immigrants who had come over from Ireland to build or to work on the railways. Seemingly they were not always welcome in 'posh' Roman Catholic churches (muddy boots, shabby clothing, lack of education?).

The absence of Irish labourers among the workers in *RTP* has been commented on; while Hastings might not have been the first destination of many Irish emigrants, nevertheless it is certain that there were some there and this is confirmed by the archive note on Fr. O'Callaghan.

BALLOONING

An unusual and slightly obscure Irish link arises from Robert's essay on airships, where he gives details of the first balloon flights in the 1780s. One event which he cites is the flight across the English Channel by Frenchman Jean Pierre Blanchard on 7th January 1785, the first sea crossing by balloon. Robert probably did not know that on 4th January 1785, a fellow Irishman, Richard Crosbie, attempted to make the first sea crossing by balloon, the first international flight in effect. Crosbie planned to set out from Ranelagh, not far from where Robert was born, and a suburb in which Samuel Croker lived in the 1860s. Crosbie's first attempt failed and he tried again on 19th January. He succeeded in making a short flight on that occasion – the first manned balloon flight in Ireland – but only across the city. Later in the same year he set out again from Dublin but after a few hours of flying he came down in the Irish Sea and was rescued. His schemes were daring and even foolhardy and his star shone over Dublin for a period of only two years, 1784 to 1786, those heady years at the dawn of human flight, but he did not achieve his aim.

Crosbie was one of the first balloonists to claim that he could direct and control a balloon so that a course could be followed and that the balloon would not be at the mercy of the winds. Robert's essay identifies this as a crucial feature of the new airships of the early 20th century. Like Robert Noonan, Crosbie was a dreamer and a man with a grand passion whose life is largely a mystery; he became an exile the America and little is known of his time there, except that he continued with his balloon obsession in New York, and was reduced to extreme poverty at the end of his days. He returned to Dublin where he died in 1824; his burial place has not been located. The achievements of both men were heroic but they are relatively unknown in their homeland.

Robert's article on airships was illustrated with his own drawings of early balloons and airships, including those of de Rozier, Blanchard and Nadar. These are copies of well-known contemporary illustrations. When Robert placed the flag with an Irish harp and the words "Erin go Bragh" (Ireland Forever) at the rear of his own model airship, he was, as pointed out by Marion Walls, linking his endeavour to the slogan and symbol of the United Irishmen

Some examples of Robert Tressell's balloon drawings. Pilatre de Rozier balloon, 1784 (left) and Jean-Pierre Blanchard's balloon, 1785.
(Reg Johnson)

of 1798 and the Transvaal Centenary celebrations of 1898. Maud Gonne designed the flag of the Irish Brigade with a harp intertwined with shamrocks on it. Robert was also, perhaps unconsciously, paying tribute to a long-standing tradition of balloon flights in Ireland. "Erin go Bragh" was a favourite balloon name and slogan for English balloonists who visited Ireland in the 19th century, a shrewd publicity and marketing slogan. When James Sadler, the first Englishman to make a balloon flight, came to Dublin in 1812 with a view to making the first crossing of the Irish Sea, one of his flags depicted the Irish harp and the words "Erin go Bragh" were inscribed on the fabric. Likewise, John Hampton also used the slogan as the name of his balloon in displays in Dublin in 1848.

Robert Noonan's model airship.
(F.C. Ball, *One of the Damned*)

THE DU CROS FAMILY IN HASTINGS

Another Irish link concerns the politician called Sir Graball D'Encloseland in *RTP*. An Irishman named William Harvey du Cros was elected as Conservative MP for Hastings in the 1906 general election, against the national swing to the Liberals. Information from Steve Peak shows that the *Hastings Mail* was disgusted at the outcome of the 1906 election and wrote as follows on 20th January 1906:

> Hastings Tories fought a political fight in 1900 and were worsted; they knew that their only chance to retrieve that disaster was to introduce a millionaire. He came and aided by powerful combinations, strange artifice, peculiar methods, his capital triumphed.

After the election, a clergyman spoke at a public meeting and harangued his listeners and berated the voters for their naivety and docility in supporting "ancient fossilated and encrusted Toryism." He went on: "I would not believe that men could be so idiotic and ignorant as to be led astray by false promises and delusive hopes. I was mistaken. I knew there were some fools in Hastings but I was unaware that they were so numerous.... Poor, deluded, benighted, infatuated, and demented Hastings." As Peak points out, these unflattering views of the voters of Hastings coincide with those of Robert Tressell in the novel, where the citizens of Mugsborough are scathingly dismissed as "composed for the most part of ignorant semi-imbeciles, slaves, slave-drivers and psalm-singing hypocrites."

Robert was politically active at the time of the 1906 election. During the campaign, he was remembered as leaning out of a window chanting: "Don't vote for either of the bounders/Throw old Thomas in the sea/Du Cros he is no good/He wants to tax your food/Socialism is the thing for you and me."

The du Cros family were of Huguenot origin and Harvey was born in Moone, Co. Kildare. He had an unhappy childhood and left home at fifteen to fend for himself. When advised to be more active for the sake of his health, he took up sports. Although in his thirties, he became a national champion at fencing and boxing; he was one of the founders of Bective Rangers rugby club and captain of the team. He had seven sons and all were involved in sports.

Harvey was on the governing body of Irish cycling and when various experiments with pneumatic tyres were being tried, he learned about the invention of Scotsman John Boyd Dunlop. He successfully sidelined Dunlop, took over the company and gave Dunlop 1,500 shares in return. This yielded very little return for the inventor, but the company made millions for Harvey and all the du Cros family. Harvey oversaw the development of motorcar tyres and helped to introduce motor taxicabs to London. (Kathleen Noonan would have empathised with the experience of John Boyd Dunlop: they both saw others benefitting enormously from what had been theirs by right, and both were cynically disposed of by sharper and more unscrupulous business minds.)

When Harvey du Cros abruptly resigned from parliament in 1908, his son Arthur replaced him as M.P. Harvey and Arthur du Cros were two archetypes of capitalism, entrepreneurs and millionaires who had amassed great wealth from their ownership of the Dunlop Rubber Company. All the family benefitted from the rubber industry with other brothers also involved in the company. Harvey returned to live in Dalkey, Co. Dublin where he died in 1918. In one obituary, he was described as "the Napoleon of the tyre industry." Arthur, the third son, was born in Blackrock, Co. Dublin in 1871, just a year after Robert Noonan. Arthur's first employment was in the civil service at the lowest grade. Like his father he was a keen sportsman, and a champion Irish cyclist. It was he who expanded the tyre business and bought large rubber plantations in Malaya.

Arthur would have had inside information on his father's intention to resign from parliament. In the short campaign of thirteen days the opposition had

Sir Arthur du Cros.
(Board of Trinity College, Dublin)

Harvey du Cros.
(Board of Trinity College, Dublin)

little time to mobilise, and Arthur won the seat. He called to Robert Noonan's home while electioneering, not realising what a hornet's nest he was stirring up in engaging in a political discussion with him. Fred Ball has an entertaining account of the meeting which he heard from Bill Gower. Robert started by quietly quizzing the candidate, going back into Irish history, while du Cros' agent impatiently stood by. Finally, Robert became more agitated until, "burning with contempt and indignation, he bade the candidate 'Good day' calling him an Irish traitor and renegade as the agent hurried him through the door."

Ironically, Arthur du Cros played an important role in the development of airships in Britain, contributing £6,000 towards the purchase of the first national airship. Innovations in flight were something which he and Robert Noonan might have discussed, had they known of each other's interests. By 1909, the potential military threat from enemy airships was causing some alarm in Britain, where there was a perception that the country was very vulnerable to an aerial attack. Arthur founded and was head of the Parliamentary Air Defence Committee, and he made what was considered an audacious proposal for the establishment of a separate air service which would not be part of the army or navy. In 1909, he was alarmed that Britain was the only European power that did not have an airship and the only one not engaged in a construction programme. He said that factories in France and Germany were capable of producing thirty airships a year and he warned that attacks were likely:

It is quite apparent that it will be possible in wartime, under certain conditions for hostile balloons to find their way over London. I know a great deal has been written in a somewhat sensational and alarmist strain on these matters and I do not wish at all to associate myself with that or to exaggerate the position at the present moment but I agree that we cannot afford to shut our eyes any longer to the fact that aerial fleets are being created on a large and comprehensive scale by foreign countries. (Quoted in Gollin, *The Impact of Air Power*, p 81-82.)

It is interesting to compare this with Robert's introduction to his essay "The Evolution of the Airship" written around 1905.

The most powerful navy that could be built, the strongest fortification that the wit of man could devise, or the most numerous and efficient army in the world, would all be comparatively helpless and at the mercy of the nation possessing a fleet of airships so designed as to be capable of carrying quantities of high explosives, and really under the control of those who manned them. Is the possibility of the construction of such an aerial fleet altogether remote – or is it on the eve of realisation?

In 1910, Arthur's father Harvey also promoted the development of airships and his brother William accompanied Clement-Bayard on the first flight of a dirigible balloon across the English Channel, when they travelled from Compiegne in France to London in just six hours. This was another historic channel crossing, echoing Blanchard's balloon crossing of 1785.

During the war, Arthur du Cros presented three motor ambulances to the War Office; they cost £50,000 and he maintained them at his own expense. He was made a baronet in 1916. He was M.P. for Hastings until 1918 and then sat for Clapham until he resigned from parliament in 1922. Arthur du Cros was not a successful businessman and became involved in what has been euphemistically termed "financial manipulation," failing to distinguish between family finances and company finances.

Surprisingly, even though the Dunlop story would have provided rich material for anti-capitalist satire, Robert makes no mention of the industrial interests of the du Cros or D'Encloseland family, nor does he mention their Irish background.

REFERENCES TO IRELAND IN *RTP*

There are few references to Ireland in the book, although there are indications that Robert had not abandoned his sense of Irishness in Hastings. Why was this aspect of his identity stifled during his political activities and in the novel? Jonathan Hyslop suggests that it was done in order to appeal more to a wider readership, as references to Ireland might have alienated him from many British readers at that time: "By excising the Irish dimension of his life from *RTP*, Noonan serendipitously increased its acceptability to a wide range of English readers."

There is only one substantial reference to Ireland in *RTP*, when Owen tries to educate his fellow workers as to the causes of poverty. One of them suggests it is over-population.

> "Overpopulation!" cried Owen, "when there's thousands of acres of uncultivated land in England without a house or human being to be seen. Is over-population the cause of poverty in France? Is over-population the cause of poverty in Ireland? Within the last fifty years the population of Ireland has been reduced by more than half. Four millions of people have been exterminated by famine or got rid of by emigration, but they haven't got rid of poverty. P'raps you think that half the people in this country ought to be exterminated as well?"

There is a passing reference later to events in Belfast and this, for all its brevity, shows that Robert was aware of events there. At the conclusion of the Great Money Trick episode, when the workers become aggressive, "the kind hearted Capitalist" threatens to call out the military to "have them shot down like dogs, the same as he had done before at Featherstone and Belfast." While Robert was living in Hastings in 1907, Big Jim Larkin, the Liverpool-born trade union organiser, was in Belfast. He mobilised the dockers and carters on a strike over union membership and united Catholic and Protestant workers in a common cause. The city was brought a standstill for four months. Even the RIC went on strike and when the military was deployed, there were riots which resulted in two men being killed in the Falls area. While the strikers ultimately went back to work in defeat, this conflict was the precursor to the dramatic events of the Lockout in Dublin in 1913, where Larkin again was leader.

Marion Walls makes an intriguing connection between the ending of *RTP* and a poem of Thomas Moore entitled "'Tis gone, and forever, the light we saw breaking." One line of the poem is "'Tis gone, and the gleams it has left of its burning, / But deepen the long night of bondage and mourning." In the last paragraph of the novel, Tressell has "Mankind awaking from the long night of bondage and mourning...." Walls traces some distinct echoes of the mood, language and tone of Moore's poem in the final pages of *RTP*.

IRISH WRITERS AND *RTP*

Fred Ball wrote to George Bernard Shaw in 1948 and although we do not have a copy of his letter, Ball noted Shaw's terse reply: "I never heard of Robert Tressell and I am not interested in him." On the other hand, Brendan Behan was familiar with Tressell's book because it was very much part of his family's reading. In *Borstal Boy* he wrote about his friendship with Tom Meadows from

Blackpool who, like Brendan, was an apprentice painter from a family of painters:

> He was a good singer, like most painters, my own family included, and the first book he'd ever heard tell of was the painter's bible, *The Ragged Trousered Philanthropists* by Robert Tressall. We had a great talk about the poor apprentice kid, 'The Walking Colour Shop', Nimrod, the old bastard of a walking foreman, and the charge hand that he was getting free drink off of most of them so as he'd keep them on, and Slyme the craw-thumper and Holy Joe, that scabbed it, and wouldn't join the Society, worked under the money and tried to rape Ruth, the young painter's new wife, when they took him in as a lodger to help them keep their new house; we spoke of poor old Jack who was old and worn out and got sent up the 60-foot ladder and was afraid to refuse in case he got sacked and himself and his old wife were put in the workhouse, so he goes up, the poor old bastard, and falls off and gets smashed to bits and his wife gets thrown into the workhouse anyway.
>
> It was our book at home too and when my mother was done telling us of the children of Lir and my father about Fionn MacCumhaill they'd come back by way of 1916 to *The Ragged Trousered Philanthropists* and on every job you'd hear painters using the names out of it for nicknames, calling their own apprentice 'The Walking Colour Shop' and, of course, every walking foreman was called Nimrod, even by painters who had never read the book, nor any other book either.

Behan was reading the abbreviated version of the book, and his reference to the attempted rape of Ruth is not an error, because that was one of the plot changes made by Jessie Pope to the original. She had Slyme assaulting Ruth who succeeds in pushing him away. Likewise, in Tressell's original text it was not Jack Linden who was killed in a fall off the ladder, but Joe Philpot. Behan's enthusiasm for the story captures the spirit in which it was read among the "brothers of the brush" and to this day, Robert Tressell and *RTP* have a special place among painters and in their union.

Irish author Dermot Bolger is another admirer of *RTP*, describing it as "a book that demands to be read." He would like it to be more widely appreciated in Ireland, but acknowledges that "its length, fervently crusading content and deliberate repetition to hammer home its message has meant that, when not being dismissed, it is generally patronised in literary circles." (*Irish Times*, 1st March 2004.)

In a surprise discovery in recent times, it was found that *RTP* was among the books read in prison in Northern Ireland. Republican prisoners in the Maze were not allowed books for some years but still managed to acquire a secret library. Among the political and historical books found in the prison after it closed was *RTP*. One republican prisoner recalled how, after he had read the first hundred pages, the book was discovered and confiscated; it was not until his release five years later that he was able to resume reading. Interestingly, a copy of *RTP* was also being read in the Loyalist wing of the prison. (Kirsty Scott, "Men of Letters, Men of Arms," *The Guardian*, 2nd December 2000.)

OTHER IRISH EMIGRANT WRITERS

Noonan was not the only Irish writer in Britain in the early 20th century focussing on the dispossessed on the margins of society. Pádraic Ó Conaire from Galway was working in London and his book *Deoraíocht*, on the theme of exile, was published in 1910. Donegal writer Patrick MacGill, "the navvy poet," had already made his name by then and his autobiographical novel *Children of the Dead End* was published in 1914. It told of the harsh conditions experienced by Irish emigrants in Scotland. By coincidence, around that time, James Joyce concluded protracted negotiations about his book *Dubliners* with Grant Richards, who published it in June 1914. Joyce got a better deal from him than Kathleen Noonan did: 10 per cent of all sales after the first 500 copies, according to Dave Harker. However, Harker adds the information that by 1915 sales of *RTP* were eight times higher than those of *Dubliners*.

WHAT IF......?

It is worth speculating briefly on what might have occurred had Robert chosen to return to Dublin rather than settle in Hastings in 1901. Would he have revived his association with John MacBride who married Maud Gonne, to the dismay of poet William Butler Yeats? Or would he have met Arthur Griffith and written for his newspaper *United Ireland*, or perhaps collaborated with Griffith in the founding of the first Sinn Féin party in 1905? He might then have associated with some of the nationalist figures who planned the 1916 Rising.

He would certainly have been outraged and appalled by the shocking living conditions of the poor of Dublin's tenements. He would surely have allied himself with the work of James Larkin, a kindred spirit, who saw himself as on a "divine mission of discontent." Larkin shared the outrage of Tressell at how workers were treated by the system and he too expressed himself in biblical language, saying he was "engaged in a holy work" and that "Christ will no longer be crucified in Dublin by these men," referring to employers.

Robert might have crossed paths with the young Sean O'Casey who later depicted life in the Dublin tenements so graphically and movingly in several plays. He might even have produced a novel of the Dublin tenements, such as *Strumpet City*, which was to be written by James Plunkett in 1969.

9 Samuel Croker

FOLLOWING THE DISCOVERY of the Croker background and the information gleaned by Fred Ball on his visit to Ireland, an amazing story of a double life emerged. Samuel was born around 1790 in Woodview, Co. Waterford. The Crokers were a family of Devon origins who were granted lands in the south of Ireland in Tudor times. The best known branch was in Ballinagarde, Co. Limerick. There is a story that when one owner of Ballinagarde was dying, he was being comforted by a clergyman who assured him that he was going to a better place; the old man cast his eye around his property, declared "I doubt it" and promptly expired. The catchphrase "I doubt it, says Croker" is still used in Limerick today.

Nick Reddan, an Australian genealogist who has done comprehensive research on the Crokers, has an on-line history of the family which runs to 180 pages. Some prominent public figures with the surname Croker were contemporaries of Samuel. John Wilson Croker (1780 – 1857) of Galway was a statesman and author; one of Samuel's sons was also named John Wilson. Thomas Crofton Croker (1798-1854) of Cork was an antiquarian and writer. Neither of these was closely related to Samuel. Nor was Richard "Boss" Croker (1843-1922), a notorious Tammany Hall politician in New York, who was born in Co. Cork and who died at his home in Glencairn, Co. Dublin.

Samuel was not titled and the memory of "Sir Samuel" is inaccurate. Neither was he in the army. He became a member of the Constabulary in 1823, not yet known as the Royal Irish Constabulary (RIC) as that was not the official title until 1867. Jim Herlihy's work on RIC Officers and men provides details of his career in the police. Some of his postings as a policeman included Dungarvan (1826) and Kilmacthomas (1834) in Co. Waterford and Carrickbeg in Co. Tipperary. He later became a stipendiary magistrate and worked in Ennis, Co. Clare until 1843. He retired in 1843 with two pensions, one of £400 a year and the other of £36. 10 shillings. From 1864 to 1869 he lived in Ranelagh, Dublin, first at No.6 Sandford Place, and from 1866 to 1869, at No.28 Sandford Road. From 1870 to 1874, he lived at No.1 Winslow Terrace in Rathgar. These were substantial houses in fashionable suburbs of Dublin. The rateable valuations of No.28 Sandford Road and No.1 Winslow Terrace were £25 and £39 respectively, indicating that even in his seventies, Samuel was prosperous enough to move to a bigger house.

The name Samuel Croker, retired resident magistrate, appeared in the press occasionally, but not in any detailed reports. On 30th September 1859, he is listed as supporting a campaign for a packet station for America via Galway, described by the *Irish Times* as "this great national undertaking, which is nothing short of patriotic." In 1868, his name appears in two lists, although without the appellation of a retired resident magistrate. One is a list of attendees at a meeting of the Conservative electors of the city of Dublin (13th November), and the other a meeting of the Central Protestant Defence Association, where he is included among those unctuously described as "the noblemen and gentlemen of the highest distinction in

No.28 Sandford Road as it looks today (on right).

the country." (6th February). Samuel Croker of Kilmacthomas is also listed as a subscriber to Samuel Lewis' *Topographical Dictionary of Ireland*, published in 1836. Another Samuel Croker also appears in newspapers occasionally, with an address in Hollyhill, Co. Cork. A passing reference in *The Freeman's Journal* of 10th May 1853 under the heading "Common Pleas Nisi Prius" lists a seduction case between a Mary Birney and a Samuel Croker but there are no further details on the case or on either of them.

SAMUEL CROKER'S FIRST FAMILY

Samuel Croker married Jane Usher (sometimes written as Ussher) Quin in September 1827 and they had five children:

> Samuel, born in 1828 in Dungarvan, Co. Waterford, died in Dungarvan in 1834
> Anne Elizabeth, born in 1829 in Dungarvan
> Arthur, born c.1832
> John Wilson, born c.1834 in Carrick-on-Suir, Co. Tipperary
> Samuel, born c.1836
> Melian, born c.1844

Jane was daughter of Arthur Quin of Dungarvan, Co. Waterford, where Samuel was stationed as a policeman. It was a custom in Ireland that when a child died, the forename would be given again to a subsequent child, hence the two sons named Samuel. These six children were born in various parts of Ireland, reflecting Samuel's postings, and some of the births were announced in the press. From 1870, the year Robert was born, Samuel and his wife Jane and their daughter Anne lived at No.1 Winslow Terrace, Rathgar (now No.49 Terenure Road East). Samuel is listed at that address in *Thom's Directory* up to 1874, and "Mrs. Croker" only is listed after that, from 1875 to 1880. Samuel is also found in *Thom's Directory* for several years under the alphabetical "List of the Nobility, Gentry, Merchants and Traders, Public Offices etc. etc. in the City of Dublin and Suburbs."

John Croker went to Liverpool where he became a ship owner. Melian married Richard Millington and lived in Birmingham. Arthur became a Surgeon-Major in the army, based at different locations in Ireland and England. It was interesting to discover that Samuel Croker had two sons and two grand-children who lived in Hastings at different times: Arthur Croker lived there on one of his military postings and his son was born there on 30th October 1876. Their address was No.25 St. Helen's Road. (*Medical Times and Gazette*, Vol. 2, 1876). I do not know how long Arthur and his family spent in Hastings, but he retired from the army on temporary half-pay in November 1878. (*London Gazette*, 13th December 1878.)

SAMUEL CROKER JUNIOR

At an early stage of this research, I was inclined to the view that the father of Robert Noonan was much more likely to have been Samuel Croker junior, who was 34 in 1870, rather than Samuel senior, who was 80 in 1870. I imagined that Samuel senior might have supported Mary Noonan as a way of covering up for the behaviour of his errant son. When I found this news item in the digital archive of the *Irish Times* (13th June 1885), it seemed to give plausibility to this theory, revealing just such a wayward son. When I first read this I had not yet discovered any details of the younger Samuel's wife's maiden name, and I thought that the Mrs. Croker here mentioned might have been Mary Noonan.

A Sad Case: A young man named Samuel Croker residing at 26 Cambridge Road, Rathmines, who, it was stated, was the son of a resident magistrate and at one time occupied a good position with the Bank of Ireland was brought into custody in the Dublin Police Court charged by his wife with having assaulted her. Mrs. Croker stated that the prisoner threw a tumbler and an iron ring at her. She wanted to have the prisoner kept away from her as she could not live with him. He was taking the things out of the house and selling them. Mr. O'Donel asked what was the prisoner? Mrs. Croker said that he was nothing at present but at one time he held a good position with the Bank of Ireland. He was of a roving disposition and had at one time gone to Australia and returned again in poverty and squandered any little property they had. She had great difficulty keeping the things in the house at all. The prisoner who appeared to have recently been drinking heavily, asked to be forgiven, promising to do whatever his wife wished in future. Mr O'Donel said the charges were too serious. Prisoner – Do for the sake of my father who you know. Mr. O'Donel – Who was your father? Prisoner – Mr. Croker, Resident Magistrate. Mr. O'Donel said that he would remand the prisoner for a week so that inquiries could be made about him in the meantime.

Unfortunately, I could discover no information on any subsequent proceedings and can only imagine that the affair was quietly disposed of. As this report was from the year when young Robert was fifteen, I briefly speculated that this incident was the last straw for him and was the cause of his leaving home and Ireland at sixteen and having no further contact with either of his parents. However, it soon became evident that this hypothesis was not sustainable and that it was the older Samuel who was recorded as Robert's father. Still, Robert's half brother Samuel was an interesting character who had quite a colourful life.

Young Samuel's wife was Josephine Johnston. Their marriage in Dublin was recorded in *The Times* of 26th January 1861: "Samuel Croker, youngest son of Samuel Croker, Esq. to Josephine Johnston of Dovegrove, King's County" (Co. Offaly today). It was published almost two months after the wedding, which was recorded as taking place on 22nd November 1860. However, church records give different details: Samuel Croker and Josephine Johnston, both of Alboro Cottage, Amiens St., were married on 25th November 1859, as recorded on the website http://churchrecords.irishgenealogy.ie. Josephine was the grand-daughter of Francis Whyte Esq., of Redhills, Co. Cavan. Samuel junior had an address of Parsonstown, King's Co. (now Birr, Co. Offaly) in a legal document of 1874 and that same address is given for him in a subscription list for the relief of sufferers by the Indian Mutiny listed in *The Times* on 1st April 1858, before his marriage.

Thom's Directory for Dublin in 1885 lists Samuel Croker Esq. as resident of No.26 Cambridge Road, Rathmines, but in 1884 and in 1886 the house was listed as vacant. As well as spending some time in Australia, Samuel junior also lived in Brandon, Manitoba, Canada at some period, according to Letters of Administration of his estate, which also show that he left £91. 5s. 6d. Samuel junior died in 1889, when his address was No.146 Upper Abbey St., Dublin. (Nick Reddan states that he joined the police in the year 1846, but this is probably an error, as there is no other evidence that he was in the police. The date is certainly inaccurate, as he was born in 1836.)

The Croker grave in Mount Jerome Cemetery in Dublin has a headstone which records the burials there of three members of the family. It reads:

In loving memory of Annie Elizabeth daughter of the late Samuel Croker
Esq. RM who departed this life on Easter Day 1880.
Also of Jane Usher Croker relict of the last mentioned, who departed this life
on 22nd Jan 1887, much lamented.

Also of Samuel Croker son of the above Samuel and Jane U. Croker
who died on the first of Jan 1889.

The Mount Jerome plot was bought by Arthur who was living in Basingstoke in 1887. According to a press report, Jane Usher Croker died at No.32 London Grove, Prince's Park, Liverpool, an address which may have been that of her son John.

There was a rift in the Croker family in the early 1870s, as recorded in the next chapter, and Samuel senior went to live in London where he died on 6th January 1875. His burial place has not yet been located, nor has any reference to a will, either in Ireland or in Britain. The rift arose out of his financial provision for Mary Noonan, which, not surprisingly, was objectionable to his first family, although the two references to him on the headstone in Mount Jerome suggest that he was not completely disowned or forgotten by them. The complexities of the familial and financial arrangements of Samuel senior, and his relationship with Mary Noonan, are discussed in the next chapter.

Croker grave in Mount Jerome.

SAMUEL CROKER fathered six children between 1828 and 1844, when he was aged between thirty-eight and fifty-four, and went on to have seven more children with Mary Noonan. Samuel started a second family when the youngest of his first family was fourteen. Robert, the author of *RTP*, was the second youngest of the children of Samuel and Mary Anne Noonan.

As collated by family historian Fíona Tipple in Appendix 1, records show that Samuel and Mary were the parents of:

> Mary Jane (Jennie), born in 1858 in Athlone, Co. Westmeath
> Henry John, born in 1860 in Dublin
> Teresa, born in 1862, in Dublin
> Ellie (Zellah) born c. 1866 "at sea"
> Adelaide Ann, born in 1867 in Dublin
> Robert, born in 1870 in Dublin
> William, born in 1872 in Dublin.

These seven children were born when their father, Samuel Croker, was between the ages of sixty-eight and eighty-two, although there is an element of doubt about the identity of William's parents. Mary Jane's name at baptism was recorded as Noonan, and the others were given the surname Croker, but their parents were not married. It is possible that Mary came from Athlone, but there is no information to connect Samuel to the town.

Robert's sisters Adelaide and Mary Jane were both living in Hastings at the same time as he was. Fred Ball also mentions a sister Ellie who lived in Liverpool, but with whom Robert seems to have had no contact when he lived there in his last months. Ball noted that Robert might have had two brothers, but he gave no further information on them, and he did not mention another sister. No information has been discovered about William or Teresa. It is possible that they did not survive into adulthood, but another brother, Henry John, has been traced by Fíona Tipple. He married Kate Manley in Bournemouth in 1883 and he gave his father's name as Samuel Noonan, Gentleman, deceased. Henry gave his age as twenty-one when he was actually twenty-three. Henry and Kate had eleven children. He was living in Great Marlow, Buckinghamshire in the 1891 census, and he died in Holland Park, London in 1935. There has previously been no mention of him in Robert Noonan's story and there appears to have been no contact between him and

Robert while the latter lived in Hastings. However, Henry was known to the Meiklejons, because John Bean Meiklejon was a witness at his wedding in 1883. Yet another family secret, it seems.

In Robert Noonan's baptismal record in St. Kevin's Church on 26th April, the parents were named as Samuel Croker and Mary Noon (sic), and the two sponsors were Michael Noon and Maria Johannah Croker. The identity of the former is not known but the latter could have been Mary and Samuel's eldest daughter Mary Jane, aged twelve. The priest, Jacobus Baxter, noted "Pater a Catholicus," meaning Samuel was not a Catholic. Mary Noon gave her address as No.37 Wexford St.

Robert Noonan had six siblings but as an adult he had regular contact with only two, Adelaide and Mary Jane. He appears to have had no contact with his mother after he left Ireland. He was secretive about his early life, and his sisters equally so. Apart from the interchanging names of Noonan and Croker used by Robert, the confusion over names persisted into his daughter Kathleen's time, when she was known to Jessie Pope as Croker and Noonan, and later chose to use a fictitious stage name, Lynne.

There are strange features in the records of the births of the Croker/Noonan children. Mary gave her surname as Noon when Robert was baptised. The parents of Mary Jane, their first-born, are given as Samuel Nonan (*sic*) and Maria Croker in baptism records. Disregarding the probable transcription error in the spelling of Noonan, they appear to have interchanged their surnames. Was this to conceal their identities, but not entirely? Or was it simply a recording error? Many years later, Mary Jane would give her father's name as Samuel Noonan when she married John Bean Meiklejon in London in 1875 at the age of sixteen. Ellie, their fifth child, also gave Samuel Noonan as her father's name when she married William Maguire in Liverpool in 1892, as did Henry John when he married Kate Manley in 1883.

In the registration of William's birth at No.25 George's Place in 1872, Mary Croker, formerly Nolan, is recorded as the mother's name. This seems to be yet another variation on Noonan. Another odd feature of William's birth details is that the father, Samuel Croker, is described as a sailor. The possibility that this record relates to a different couple named Samuel Croker and Mary Croker, née Nolan, cannot be discounted, but seems unlikely. It is more likely that it is another case of official obfuscation by the parents. No further information on William has been found.

The website http://churchrecords.irishgenealogy.ie has details of the baptisms of Henry, Teresa, Adelaide and Robert. In all cases, Samuel Croker is the father, but in Teresa's case, the mother's name is incorrectly given as "Maria Moran." In fact, the original record shows Noonan, but the name has been incorrectly transcribed, so this apparent name change is not related to any effort by Mary to conceal her identity. Henry and Teresa were baptised in St. Mary's Pro-Cathedral and Adelaide in St. Michan's.

No.	Date and Place of Birth.	Name (if any).	Sex.	Name and Surname and Dwelling-place of Father.	Name and Surname and Maiden Surname of Mother.	Rank or Profession of Father.	Signature, Qualification, and Residence of Informant.	When Registered.	Signature of Registrar.	Baptismal Name, if added after Registration of Birth, and Date.
341	Twentieth January 1872 25 Georges Place	William	male	Samuel Crotter 25 Georges Place	Mary Crotter formerly Nolan	Sailor	Mary Crotter mother 25 Georges Place	February thirteenth 1872	JR Ferguson Registrar	

Birth details of William, born on 20th January 1872, showing Mary Croker, formerly Nolan, as his mother and Samuel described as a sailor.

ADDRESSES FOR MARY NOONAN

The addresses recorded for Mary Noonan illustrate a high degree of mobility. Her first child Mary Jane was born in 1858 in Preaching Lane, Athlone, Co. Westmeath, 123km from Dublin. The next birth was that of Henry John in 1860, when Mary's address was No.47 Montgomery St., Dublin. For Teresa's birth in 1862, she was in No.18 Mabbot St., Dublin. Ellie was born in 1866 "at sea" according to her entry on censuses of 1891 and 1911. For Adelaide Ann's birth in 1867, Mary was in No.53 Lower Wellington St. For Robert's birth in 1870, her address was No.37 Wexford St. and for William's birth in 1872, she was in No. 25 George's Place, off Dorset St.

This pattern of mobility seems unusual, and it is reminiscent of Robert's many addresses in Hastings. If Ellie was correct in later life in recording her birth "at sea," it can only refer to the Irish Sea and Mary must have travelled to England at some stage – yet another puzzle. But it could also be that Ellie's birth was not recorded and that "at sea" was a way of explaining this absence of any record of her birth.

Preaching Lane, Athlone today.

According to a legal document of 1873, Mary was in No.38 Bessborough Avenue, North Strand in that year. This is one address at which Robert must have lived, if he was in his mother's care, as he was just three years old. There are some remarkable aspects to the family situation of Samuel Croker and Mary Noonan. Despite giving the same address for birth registration purposes, it is not known whether he ever lived with Mary, or how he managed to maintain two households in Dublin, or what either household knew of the other. Mary was a Catholic and Samuel was a Protestant. As an unmarried mother of several children, she would have been judged as giving scandal, and would have not have been in good standing in a parish. There was a significant age gap between Mary and Samuel; if she was eighteen, for example, when she had her first child with Samuel, she would have been only thirty in 1870. He was certainly more than twice her age. It should be noted that it might have been in Samuel's interests that the name changes were made on the birth records: as a public figure of some standing, he may have been at pains to conceal any information which might cause a scandal or which might lead to conflict with his wife and family. By 1873, however, the secret was out, as revealed in legal documents.

DOCUMENTS OF 1873 AND 1874 IN REGISTRY OF DEEDS, DUBLIN

After his visit to Dublin, Fred Ball was sent a summary of two legal documents from the Registry of Deeds in Henrietta St. He did not read the documents but published this summary as he received it. All subsequent biographers of Robert have relied on this for information, rather than the documents themselves. The first document recorded various provisions made by Samuel for Mary in 1873, including the information that he demised (i.e. granted) her a house on Great Britain St. which produced an annual rental income of over £27. The second document was a family settlement between the members of Samuel's first family and reveals considerable ill-feeling among them towards him. Full details of these two documents are in Appendix 2 and Appendix 3.

Fortunately, Fred Ball provided exact references for the documents. Following the wise advice of Fíona Tipple, I read the originals of the two legal documents in the Registry of Deeds, and discovered that the report sent to Ball did not give the complete picture. The summary was factually accurate, but it omitted to state that the settlement of 1874 arose out of a dispute over the terms of two documents of 1873, that questions had been raised about the legality of his 1873 provisions for Mary, or that the 1874 settlement contained clear threats of repercussions for any of his first family who challenged his settlement to Mary.

This is the relevant information from the first document, that of 11th August 1873:

A memorial of a deed of conveyance bearing date the 11th day of August, 1873 and made between Samuel Croker of No.1 Winslow Terrace, Rathgar in the County of Dublin Esq. of the one part and Mary Anne Noonan of No.38 Bessborough Avenue, North Strand in the County of Dublin, spinster, of the other part.....

the said Samuel Croker granted and conveyed unto the said Mary Noonan her heirs and assigns all that brick house with the back side and garden thereunto belonging situate lying and being in Great Britain St. (now numbered 145).....

The following information comes from the second document, dated 2nd June 1874. This was made between Samuel, his wife Jane and the adult offspring of his first family. It is noteworthy that Samuel was then living in London, although no actual address was given. It opens as follows:

A memorial of a deed of family settlement bearing date of 2nd June 1874 and made between Samuel Croker at present residing in London in the Co. of Middlesex in England, retired Resident Magistrate....

The other parties are his wife Jane, sons John, Arthur, Samuel and daughters Annie and Melian and also Melian's husband, Richard Millington. The document continues:

That by a certain indenture dated the 11th August 1873 the said Samuel Croker granted to one Mary Noonan an annuity of £100 payable out of his said pensions and by another deed of the same date granted to her the said premises in Great Britain St. hereinafter described and reciting that questions were raised as to the validity of the said two last mentioned deeds and that to settle this and all other differences the memorializing settlement had been entered into.

As there is no mention of the annuity of £100 in the surviving deed of 1873, which concerns the property on Great Britain St. only, clearly there was another document of the same date granting the annuity. The 1874 document continues:

It was further witnessed that all the said parties thereto witnessing themselves respectively and for the respective heirs, executors, admors and assigns ratified and confirmed said two indentures of the 11th day of August 1873 and should any of them commence any legal proceedings whatsoever for the purpose of impeaching said two indentures or take any steps to prevent or hinder the said Samuel Croker from residing where he chose that then the memorializing deed was to cease and be absolutely null and void.

The document goes on to assign to John, as trustee, a mortgage to the value of £300, the house at No.1 Winslow Terrace with its contents and land, and lands and buildings at Irvine Castle, the location of which is not specified. (Ball later found information to suggest that it might have been Inverin Castle rather than Irvine Castle. Irvine Castle could relate to Irvinestown, Co. Fermanagh and Inverin is in Co. Galway. No further information on either of these properties has been located.)

The 1874 document reads like a final settlement for Samuel's first family and a clear confirmation of his wish to settle property and income on Mary Noonan. Clearly someone in the first family had challenged his earlier provision for her and he shows a firm determination to prevent any change to his earlier grant of an annuity and of property to her.

Could this be a testament to a long and on-going love affair with Mary after having seven children together? While his pension was only for his life, the property he granted to Mary would have provided her with security and a rental income. The document shows that Samuel was supporting Mary, and presumably their children, and the assumption must be that he had been providing for them before this time also.

SAMUEL'S DEATH IN LONDON, JANUARY 1875

It is interesting that according to the second document Samuel had concerns about his freedom to live where he chose to. He had left Ireland to live in London by June 1874. What had happened to cause this rupture with his wife and first family in his last years? Had Jane and their children just discovered his liaison with Mary Noonan? Or had their patience finally run out, after learning of yet another child fathered by him in 1872? Did they try to prevent him leaving Dublin? Were they conscious of their father's advancing age and the necessity of securing their inheritances?

In January 2014, Fíona Tipple made a very significant discovery: a record of Samuel's death in London on 6th January 1875. His address was 91 East India (Dock) Road and the cause of death was given as debility, old age. His age was recorded as eighty-six. The informant, who was in attendance at his death, was "M.J. Noonan" described as a grand-daughter, who lived at the same address. This probably was Mary Jane, the first child he had with Mary Noonan in 1858. Why would she have described herself as his grand-daughter? Was it to explain the obvious disparity – approximately seventy years – in their ages? Or to explain their different surnames? Or was this an indication that Samuel was not actually her father and that she was aware of that? Nevertheless, in her marriage certificate of the same year, she named Samuel as her father, giving him the surname Noonan. It looks like another example of concealment, and it echoes Jessie Pope's letter in which she said that Kathleen told her that Samuel Croker was her *great*-grandfather.

There is nothing in the death certificate to indicate whether any other members of the Noonan family were present at Samuel's death. There was a family story of Robert spending some time in England in his childhood, as recalled by Kathleen. Could it be that Robert and other family members went with Samuel, and perhaps Mary, to London around this time, after Samuel had left his first family? Could it be that Samuel and Mary spent a short time in London together until his death and that Mary then returned with the children to Dublin? Robert did state in South Africa in 1897 that his last country of residence was Ireland, but it is noteworthy that all of the Noonan children that we know of eventually ended up living in England.

Before the discovery of the death certificate, I had speculated that if Samuel had gone alone to London, then there was a parallel between his last days and those of Robert. Both men left the place where they had family members, and went off to a strange city to die within months. The information that he had at least one familiar person with him meant that his death was not as lonely as Robert's would be in 1911.

This was likely to have been Mary Jane's second time signing an official record, if she was indeed the sponsor "Maria Johannah Croker" at Robert's birth. Mary Jane, the eldest of the Noonan children, seems to have carried many of the family secrets: she was with Samuel when he died in London, and she knew that her brother Henry John had married in England, but it seems that this information may not have been passed on to Alice, or at least was not divulged to Fred Ball, or to Kathleen. The secrets of the Noonan family ran deep and, in the light of this new information, Alice's remark to Fred Ball that "the whole subject of family history was taboo" takes on an added significance.

Having speculated much on the relationship between Samuel and Mary, and having found no clear resolution, I had a further task, which was to check in *Thom's Directory* for all those addresses at which Mary Noonan lived, according to birth records of six of her seven children, in order to obtain a clearer picture of the kind of areas in which she lived. This property trail led me to discoveries which add even more mystery to her story.

MARY NOONAN'S RESIDENCES IN DUBLIN

The little information available to Robert's biographers about Mary Noonan came largely from Kathleen, who told Fred Ball what she recalled from her childhood. Mary was said to have been frivolous and vain, proud of her dainty hands and feet. The Robert Tressell Family Papers contain what appears to be an unlikely story from Kathleen, recounted by Marion Walls, that on one occasion at a ball, Mary kept her partner busy picking up her fan and her handkerchief, until he called a footman and told him to pick up anything she dropped. Mary was also said to have arranged a marriage for her eldest daughter at sixteen, because she did not like having a daughter that old, as it dated her.

In reality, these tales tell us nothing for certain about Mary Noonan and may be no more than half-remembered stories told to an impressionable child.

The address for Mary Noonan in 1860, when Henry John was born, was No.47 Montgomery St. and when Teresa was born in 1862, it was No.18 Mabbot St. Both of these were very close to each other on the north side of the Liffey, near the railway station at Amiens St., now called Connolly Station. In 1860, Nos.46 to 48 Montgomery St. were listed in *Thom's Directory* simply as "tenements" with no occupants' names. In 1861 and 1862, Nos.47 to 49 Montgomery St. were listed as tenements. Out of 74 buildings listed on the street, 48 were described as tenements. There was commercial activity on the street also, with grocery and spirit dealers, a saw-mill, a lodging-house, a dairy, a coachmaker and a shoemaker.

No.18 Mabbot St. was also listed as a tenement in 1862. Out of seventy-one houses on the street, twenty-four were described as tenements. There were several tradesmen and craftsmen on the street, including a shoemaker, a bacon curer, a carpenter, an upholsterer, a bricklayer, a cork manufacturer, a printer and a bookbinder.

The address of No.53 Lower Wellington St., given by Mary in 1867 when Adelaide was born, was recorded as occupied by a Mrs. Moore for several years. On that street, there were eight tenement houses out of seventy-one listed. In 1870, when Robert was born, Mary gave the address as No.37 Wexford St., and according to *Thom's Directory*, the occupant was David Daly, surgeon, whose name had been listed for a few years before then. In 1871, the building was occupied by John Staunton and was described as "dining rooms." Most houses on Wexford St. were commercial premises, with only one a tenement. Close to No.37 were a provisions dealer, a nail and leather seller, a dairy, a chandler and a miller/baker. There were no tenements listed in George's Place, Mary's address when William was born in 1872.

DUBLIN SLUMS

By 1900, the slums of inner city Dublin were notorious dens of poverty and deprivation. This was the culmination of a pattern of decline which began early in the 19th century, after the Act of Union, when Dublin lost its status as the second city of the empire. Over time, the graceful Georgian mansions became teeming tenements and the wealthy moved to the suburbs. Jacinta Prunty's study of Dublin's slums begins with this overview: "The slum question in Dublin 1800-1925 revolved around a number of key issues: contagious disease, poor sanitation, tenement accommodation, overcrowding and moral degradation, vagrancy and homelessness, and the policing, control and relief of the poor by both state and charity organisations."

The Montgomery St./Mabbot St. area of Dublin city was a notorious part of the city through the mid and late 19th century and up until the 1920s. The

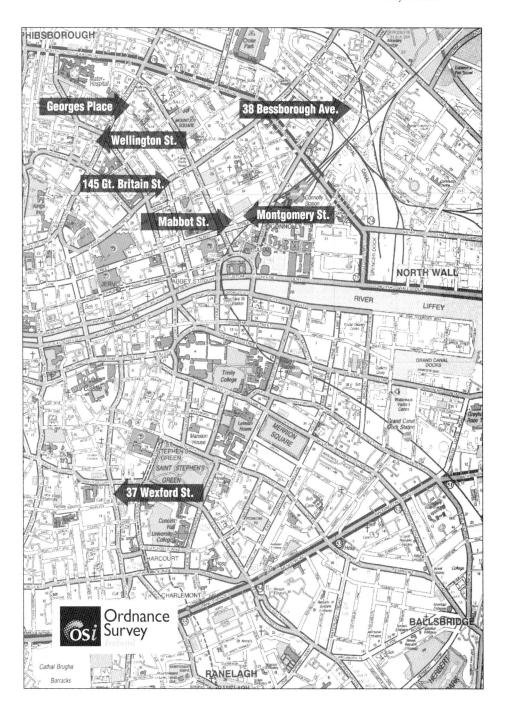

Dublin addresses associated with Mary Noonan.
(Ordnance Survey Ireland Permit No. 8931 © Ordnance Survey Ireland/Government of Ireland)

area was a by-word for poverty and deprivation, for vice and prostitution, for squalor and disease. It was the red-light district, known as "Monto," from Montgomery. Other streets with a reputation for being the location of brothels were the nearby Mecklenburgh St., Beaver St. and Purdon St. Jacinta Prunty describes the Mecklenburgh/Montgomery district as "a most extensive brothel area." Maria Luddy wrote that around 1900, "the Mecklenburg/Montgomery district of the city, north-east of the Custom House, marked the infamous Monto district…. The nearby Mabbot St. was also notorious because many houses there were brothels." It must be noted however that these observations refer to a period over thirty years after Mary Noonan was living in Montgomery St. and Mabbot St. Nevertheless, the reputation of the area in the 1860s was similar, although it is worth noting that it was also an area where the cheapest lodgings could be found, especially for somebody new to the city – like Mary Noonan, for example, who had come from Athlone.

THE *DEMI-MONDE* OF MONTO

Not every house in Mabbot St. and Montgomery St. was a brothel and not every woman living in the area was a prostitute. In 1886, the residents of Upper Mecklenburgh St, who described themselves as "respectable working classes" succeeded in having their street re-named Tyrone St., but their efforts to shake off the stigma of the old name were ineffective, because the lower and more notorious end was then renamed Lower Tyrone St. In 1911, the upper part became Waterford St. and the lower part Railway St. Parts of Montgomery St. were cleared in 1905 and it was re-named Foley St. after the celebrated sculptor John Henry Foley who was born on the street in 1818. (The original name for Montgomery St. in the early 18th century was the evocative "World's End Lane".) Mabbot St. became Corporation St. and is now James Joyce St.

None of these early name changes made any difference to the reputation of the area and it was not until the 1920s that the brothels were finally cleared away. James Joyce wrote about Monto in *Ulysses*. He calls it "Nighttown" and Bella Cohen's was based on the notorious brothels run by Becky Cooper and Eliza Mack, which Joyce is believed to have visited. Joyce wrote:

> The Mabbot street entrance to Nighttown, before which stretches an uncobbled tramsiding set with skeleton tracks, red and green will-o'-the-wisps and danger signals. Rows of flimsy houses with gaping doors. Rare lamps with rainbow fans.

Terry Fagan's folk history of Monto gives many details of life in the area which Mary Noonan would have recognised. Dublin was unusual among European cities in the late 19th century in that the authorities tolerated the practice of prostitution and there were no raids or closures of brothels – many of the

A scene in Monto in the early 1900s

Some of the older street names survive today

clients were policemen themselves and the area was also known for its shebeens or drinking dens.

There were three kinds of brothels. At the top of the scale were the "fancy houses" which were frequented by the wealthiest clients. These would come at night in hansom cabs with drawn curtains. The houses were lavishly decorated and furnished, with doormen controlling entry, and inside was a parlour with a piano and rooms where a medical certificate over the bed "guaranteed" that the women were disease free. The certificates were obtained from clients who were doctors or medical students. The women dressed well and would often tour the city in open carriages drawing attention to their services and they would make sure to be seen on Grafton Street, at the Horse Show and at race meetings. When regiments were visiting Dublin barracks the women would leave their calling cards and sometimes provided transport to Monto for clients.

The second class of brothel was for lower professional classes such as clerks and shop assistants and the third class for soldiers and sailors. These imitated some of the features of the higher class brothels. However, the women were older, the furnishing less lavish, and the conditions less hygienic. Rooms could also be rented in the area for prostitutes to bring men to. Naturally, with no police interest in the area, robberies of clients and other crimes were common.

The madams of Monto were notorious, as were the "fancy men" who acted on their behalf as bodyguards and procurers. If a woman became pregnant, she was of no further use and the madams would abandon such women to their own fate. Many of the girls came from a rural background and may first have been lured into brothels with the promise of well-paid work in "domestic service." Once involved, they became trapped, although some of them found it a profitable living. Neighbours were extraordinarily charitable towards the women, often sheltering them in their own homes when they had been turned out by madams, and very often taking in and supporting their babies. Families informally adopted these children who were referred to as "Monto babies," a term which was meant as kindly and did not imply any stigma. (There is a parallel with Ruth Easton's child being absorbed into the Owen family in *RTP*.)

Maria Luddy points out that some women chose prostitution as a means of earning a living, in a society where there were few opportunities for young women to earn a living independently. Domestic service was the most common employment for women in Ireland in the late 19th century, but prostitution was a profitable alternative for some. With luck, a woman might be fortunate enough to find a wealthy man who would support her and enable her to have a better standard of living. Luddy cites one exceptional case of a woman named Laura Bell, who became very rich by the age of twenty-one through her liaison with a Nepalese man who later became prime minister of his country.

Prostitution in Ireland was often associated with soldiers and was very prevalent in towns where there were military barracks – garrison towns as they were known. Dublin was decidedly a garrison town as was Athlone. The proximity to the railway station, barracks and docks had an impact on the dark reputation of the Monto area. The nearby Aldborough House was used as a barracks during the Crimean War (1853-56) and many soldiers settled in the Monto area on their return from the war. Luddy describes prostitutes as "a generally mobile population, migrating to towns and cities" and notes that "it was common practice for women to change their names to confuse the authorities."

Whatever her personal circumstances, Mary Noonan lived for a time as an unmarried mother in the heart of a district that was notorious. All about her were women who were part of that twilight world of Monto. She may have become one of the fortunate few who were lifted out of a life of poverty by an association with a wealthy man. Samuel Croker was not outstandingly wealthy, but at least in 1873-74 he was making a generous provision for Mary. He was certainly her benefactor up to the mid-1870s and their liaison had lasted at least since 1858 in Athlone.

MARY NOONAN, PROPERTY OWNER

The evidence points to the conclusion that Mary Noonan was a kept woman, a mistress maintained by Samuel Croker and living in the red-light district of Dublin in the early 1860s, although she was gradually moving away from the north inner city enclave to better-off areas. If Montgomery St. and Mabbot St. were extremely disreputable, Lower Wellington St. was at a remove, as was

Foley St. today, formerly Montgomery St.

No.38 Bessborough Ave. today (first on right), sold by Mary Noonan in 1873.

George's Place. Wexford St. was across the city, and different in character, while Bessborough Ave. was a respectable cul-de-sac.

The last Dublin residence that we know of for Mary represented a step up in the world, a terraced cottage in a cul-de-sac. No.38 Bessborough Ave. is cited as her address in the legal document of 1873, when it was occupied by a Mrs. Kiernan, according to *Thom's Directory*. Prior to 1873, the house numbers on the avenue only went up to No.32. In 1874 and 1875, No.38 was occupied by "Mrs. Numan" according to *Thom's Directory*, and after that by a John O'Reilly. (It would not be surprising for a directory published annually to contain some inaccuracies, which could explain the spelling Numan, but the name could also be another variation of her surname provided by Mary herself.) There were no commercial buildings, no trades, no shops or services, and five occupants among the fifty-one listed were female, all with the title "Mrs."

I conducted a search of records in the Registry of Deeds in early February 2014 and made another significant discovery: a document dated 18th August 1873 recording the sale of No.38 Bessborough Ave. (Document ref: 1873.30.145.) This is the opening:

> A memorial of an assignment made the eighteenth day of August in the Year of Our Lord one thousand eight hundred and seventy three between Mary Nunan of Number 38 Bessborough Avenue in the County of the City of Dublin, spinster, of the one part and John O'Reilly of Number 13 Bessborough Avenue aforesaid, cabinet maker … in consideration of the sum of fifty pounds to the said Mary Nunan in hand paid by the said John O'Reilly, she the said Mary Nunan did grant and assign to the said John O'Reilly his executors admors and assigns all that and those that dwelling house ——— (?) or tenement situate on the south-east of Bessborough Avenue

in the parish of St. Thomas and County of the City of Dublin formerly known as Number 20 and now known as Number 38....

This document confirms the surprising fact that Mary Noonan owned this house, and sold it just seven days after Samuel Croker granted the property at No.145 Great Britain Street to her, on 11th August 1873. The solicitor involved in the sale was John Weldon of North Great George's St. The document also shows that "Mrs. Numan" in *Thom's Directory* is a mis-print for Nunan, and that the *Directory* was late in listing her as the occupant in 1874 and 1875. The change from No.20 to No.38 may have occurred when more houses were built on the road. No information has been found in the records about how Mary came to own the house. The possibility is that she was given it by Samuel, as she was given the house on Great Britain St.

No.145 Parnell St., formerly Great Britain Street, sold by Mary Noonan in 1875.

My next search in the Registry of Deeds was for information on No.145 Great Britain St. Mary's name does not appear in any editions of *Thom's Directory* in connection with this property, which could have provided another home for her and for her children after the sale of No.38 Bessborough Ave. No.145 was a substantial commercial premises of four storeys and yielded an annual rent of over £27. Along with the £100 from Samuel's pension, this gave Mary an income of over £127 for one full year at least, until Samuel's death in early 1875. Charles Callan has estimated that she would have been very comfortable on this income, the equivalent of about £2.8s.4d. per week, at a time when a skilled artisan was earning about £1. 5s. 0d. a week and a labourer was paid about 15s. a week.

However, I discovered that she chose to sell the house rather than live on the rent. Another document in the Registry of Deeds records the sale of No.145 on 1st March 1875, three months after Samuel's death. (Document ref: 1875.9.264.) This is the opening paragraph:

A memorial of a Deed of Conveyance bearing date the first day of March one thousand eight hundred and seventy five and made between Mary Noonan of East India Dock Road, London in the County of Middlesex, spinster, of the one part and William David Bradley of 32 Kenilworth Square, Rathgar in the County of Dublin Esq. of the other part....

No.145 was sold to the solicitor who acted for Samuel in 1874 and 1875, William David Bradley, and it seems that Mary was not in Dublin to conclude the sale, as only her seal and not her signature is recorded. The sale price is not included, but as the cottage at Bessborough Ave. had a rateable valuation of between £4 and £6, and sold for £50, the business premises on Great Britain St. with a valuation of £60, must have sold for at least £500. It would have taken a skilled artisan eight years to earn that amount, according to the figures provided by Charles Callan. The four-storey house at No.145 Great Britain St. was a commercial premises at ground floor, occupied by Edward Wood and Co., family grocers, general importers and wine merchants in 1874, but from 1875 it was occupied by Richan Brothers, wine merchants and family grocers.

This evidence that three months after Samuel's death, Mary was living at his London address suggests that she was with him all the time he was there. If Mary and Mary Jane were with Samuel in London, it seems likely that all the children, including Robert, were there with them. This would mean that at the age of five, Robert was in London.

A surprising discovery by Fíona Tipple just days before this book went to press opened up a whole new area of investigation regarding Mary Noonan's life after Samuel's death, and led to confirmation that Robert was indeed in London in 1881. In the marriage certificate of Mary Jane Noonan and John Bean Meiklejon of 27th December 1875, the two witnesses signed their names as Sebastian Zumball and Mary Zumball. Mary Jane was aged sixteen, and her father is named as Samuel Noonan. The address for Mary Jane and her husband was 37 Fitzroy Street, where Sebastian Zumbuhl was resident in the late 1870s, according to Electoral Registers. He was living at 27 Elmore Street in 1883, also according to Electoral Registers.

Some further details can now be added to the genealogical jigsaw of the Noonan family. In the Registration District of Poplar in the first quarter of 1875, Fíona found a marriage record of Sebastian Zumbuhl and Mary Noonan. The exact date has not yet been established, but it was within weeks of the death of Samuel Croker and in the same period as the sale of the property at No.145 Great Britain St., Dublin. Fíona also discovered that in the 1891 census, Sebastian and Mary Zumbuhl were living at No.18 Chapel Place, Liverpool. Sebastian was a Swiss cabinet maker and the couple had two sons, Sebastian Joseph and Leo. Mary gave her estimated date of birth as 1849, and her place of birth as Dublin. (This date of birth cannot be correct as Mary Jane was born in 1858.) Fíona also found death records for Sebastian (1894) and Mary (1896) in Liverpool. The children, Sebastian (1876-1915) and Leo (1878-1897), were two more half-brothers of Robert Noonan, hitherto unknown. Curiouser and curiouser!

Following this revelation, Brenda Douglas, a descendant of Ellie Noonan with an interest in family research, traced the addresses of the Zumbuhl family and made a dramatic discovery. Tracking the address No.27 Elmore Street, Finsbury, London in the census of 1881, she found that a family recorded as either Zumfield or Lumfield was living there; the handwriting is difficult to decipher on the census form. The father was Sebastian, the mother Mary, and there were three sons: Sebastian, aged five, Leo, aged two, and Robert, aged nine. Sebastian, the father, was recorded as a cabinet-maker aged thirty-two, born in Switzerland and Mary was thirty-four, born in Dublin, although she was certainly much older than that in 1881.

In spite of the rather odd version of the Zumbuhl name which appears in the census, there can be no doubt that this is Robert Noonan, living with his mother and step-father in London in 1881, and incorrectly recorded as being born in London. It is noteworthy that the surname and date confusion so familiar in the Noonan story persists in these census returns. Many more questions now arise about Robert's life, his siblings' lives and their mother's life, but they must wait for another publication. One inescapable conclusion is that Robert Noonan was a Londoner as well as a Dubliner. Two addresses at which he lived in London are No.37 Fitzroy St. and No.27 Elmore St., Finsbury. By a strange quirk of fate, No.37 Fitzroy St. had two Irish occupants in the census of 1881, when the Zumbuhl family had moved to Elmore St. – George Bernard Shaw and his mother! I am grateful to Brenda Douglas for this little gem of information. The restored house is now open to the public; it is called Fitzroy House, and it is a museum in memory of L. Ron Hubbard, founder of Scientology, who lived there in the 1950s.

The Zumbuhl family moved from London to Liverpool at some time after 1883, for reasons not known, and if Robert Noonan moved with them, then he

Mary Noonan, mother of Robert Tressell

has a claim to be called a Liverpudlian as well as a Dubliner and Londoner. More significantly, this would mean that his journey to Liverpool in the summer of 1910 was a return to a place which he would have known from childhood. It is deeply poignant to learn that Robert Noonan and his mother Mary both died in Liverpool; Mary's burial place has yet to be located, but her death is recorded in the parish register of St. Francis Xavier Catholic Church, Salisbury Street.

Robert is the only one of the Noonan children to be recorded in the Zumbuhl household in 1881 and there is no further information on the whereabouts of Ellie, Adelaide, Theresa and William in the 1870s and 1880s. Ellie and Adelaide are however recorded in the 1891 census as being in domestic service in Great Crosby near

Liverpool. 1891 was the year in which Robert was married in Cape Town.

The date of Robert's departure for Cape Town is still not known, but the most convincing evidence that Robert lived in Ireland after early childhood comes from an official document of 1897 in South Africa. It is worth looking more closely at this. The document cited by Fred Ball came from the archives of the Commissioners for Mines in Johannesburg. It registered Robert's details on arrival in Johannesburg on 15th August 1896 and incorrectly gave his date of birth as 17th April 1871. Under the heading "Last Place of Residence" the entry was "Ireland." If this is correct, Robert must have returned to live in Ireland at some time in the 1880s, before setting out for South Africa, but no evidence has yet been found to support this.

NEW INFORMATION ON MARY NOONAN AND FAMILY

1875:

Mary Noonan married Sebastian Zumbuhl in London in the first quarter of the year. Two sons: Sebastian Joseph (1876-1915) and Leo (1878-1897)

Mary Jane Noonan married John Bean Meiklejon in London on 27th December

1881 CENSUS:

Robert Noonan living with his mother Mary and her husband Sebastian Zumbuhl and their two sons, Sebastian and Leo, in No.27 Elmore Street, Finsbury, London.

1891 CENSUS:

Ellie and Adelaide Noonan in domestic service in Great Crosby, near Liverpool, in the house of a Frederick Hoyer.

Henry John Noonan living in Great Marlow, Buckinghamshire with wife Kate and children.

Mary Noonan/Zumbuhl living with husband Sebastian and two sons Sebastian and Leo in No.18 Chapel Place, Liverpool.

1894:

Sebastian Zumbuhl (senior) died in Liverpool.

1896:

Mary Noonan/Zumbuhl died in Liverpool on 23rd June 1896. Address: 18 Chapel Place. Parish register of St. Francis Xavier Catholic Church. (*England & Wales Free BMD Death Index, 1837-1915 – Ancestry.com; Liverpool, England, Catholic Burials Index 1813-1988 – Ancestry.com*)

Conclusion

A T THE END OF THIS RESEARCH, much still remains to be discovered about Robert Noonan's life between his birth in Dublin in 1870 and his marriage in South Africa in 1891. Of the Irish-born children of Mary Noonan, the five who have been traced - Mary Jane, Adelaide, Ellie, Henry and Robert - seem to have survived well. All married and had families, and one gained immortality by writing an influential and much-loved novel. More remains to be discovered about the two sons Mary had with Sebastian Zumbuhl, about Robert's life in that household, about when and why he left the family, and about why he never spoke of them.

The extraordinary life of Mary Noonan in Ireland and in England took many surprising turns. The family recollection that she re-married and that Robert did not get on with his step-father now has more plausibility and Robert may indeed have had a "fractured" childhood. If he was brought up in an unhappy home, this might explain the absence of any definite information about that period of his life and his extreme reticence and secrecy about his upbringing. The extent of his ties to Ireland is now also open to question. If he left Ireland around the age of three or four, he may not have felt any great personal bond with the city and country of his birth. His involvement in 1798 commemorations in South Africa and his passion when confronting Arthur du Cros in Hastings may have stemmed from a romantic nationalism about the country of his birth rather than any personal experience in Ireland.

On the other hand, the fact that Robert and two of his sisters kept in contact in adulthood, when they were in countries as far apart as England, South Africa and Chile, and that they eventually ended up living in the same town in the south of England shows that there was a family bond between them and that they must have had a shared past. Robert could have known little of his father Samuel, who died when he was under five. The possibility still remains that, while Mary Noonan was definitely his mother, the elderly Samuel Croker may have been a father-figure rather than his biological father. He is probably best described as "putative father."

In one last amazing discovery, Brenda Douglas has provided a photograph from her family records of a woman who is almost certainly Mary Noonan. It is a great pleasure to include a photograph of this resourceful, resilient and remarkable woman.

SAMUEL CROKER AS BARRINGTON?

In his Introduction to the Oxford World Classics edition of *RTP*, Peter Miles wisely cautions against "the biographical fallacy, the assumption that if an episode was in the novel, then it must have happened to Noonan." There is a strong temptation for biographers to read too many of the novel's incidents into the life of Robert Noonan, especially given the dearth of reliable information on his life, but it is difficult to ignore some parallels. This section offers some more speculative possibilities, in full consciousness of the licence taken. (Miles indulges in some speculation himself when he writes about Robert's nationalism: "Doubtless he had Fenian sympathies even before he left Ireland." There is no evidence to support this claim, nor to support Miles' view that "for Noonan, Britain was probably only a staging post on his way to a further life in Canada." The option of going to Canada only arose when he was in a state of great disillusionment after the rejection of the novel.)

The rather shadowy figure of Barrington plays a relatively minor role in the novel and that is mainly as a mouthpiece for socialist ideas and theory. At the end, however, his actions are significant. Barrington comes from another world, the world of wealth and privilege, and he chooses to live and work among the builders of Mugsborough to experience their lives for himself. Barrington was believed by the workers to have disgraced himself in some way and to have been disowned by his wealthy family – as Samuel Croker left his family or was disowned by them when his secret life was exposed. It was said of Barrington that "Nobody knowed exactly who 'e was or where 'e come from but anyone could tell 'e'd been a toff."

Both were from another world, mingling with people of a different class of society, part of that group but not belonging, able to withdraw to their own sphere as they wished: "I am going to pass Christmas with my own people," says Barrington. There are differences between Barrington and Croker of course: the former was in his twenties, and above all was a committed and idealistic socialist who planned to return in the spring with a socialist van to continue to spread the message in Mugsborough. Whatever Samuel Croker's beliefs were, they did not embrace socialism.

Some of the final scenes of the novel have been criticised for sentimentality and for apparently sending the message that the benevolence and generosity (philanthropy even) of the wealthy is a solution for the problems of the poor. Frank and Nora Owen are deeply concerned for their family's future, including the unwanted child of Ruth Easton, whom they have adopted. In the novel, before Barrington leaves to spend Christmas at home, he comes across their son Frankie and other children gazing longingly at the alluring toys in a shop window. Barrington plays Santa Claus, telling them that he has been sent by Santa to help them get what they wish, and he takes them into the shop where they choose their gifts.

I have an image of a wealthy outsider, an occasional visitor, well-dressed and well-spoken, with a group of children outside an attractive shop, spending money on them at Christmas time. Could Robert be recalling such an incident from his childhood, when his father treated him? Then Barrington intervenes to help Frank and Nora by giving them a gift of money. He sends young Frankie back to the house with an envelope containing £10 for the Owen family and £5 to be divided up among other needy people. Could the real Samuel Croker, who in 1873 gifted money and property to Mary Noonan, have inspired aspects of the fictional Barrington, who rescued the fortunes of the Owen family with a money gift? At the very least, they were both benefactors whose generosity changed the course of people's lives.

This resolution of their problems is a great relief to the Owens, and for Nora "all the undefined terror of the future faded away as she thought of all this small piece of paper made possible." For the reader, however, it is a *deus ex machina* resolution, another kind of "great money trick" even. It is difficult to accept that the despair and gloom of the previous days could have been dispelled in such a facile manner. It is as if an exhausted and ailing Robert Tressell was experiencing difficulty in bringing his sprawling novel to an end and chose this resolution in order finally to have it ready to submit for publication.

The final scene in the novel depicts Barrington's train passing over a railway bridge with him waving a white handkerchief, as he had promised the excited Frankie, and the Owen family waving back from the window of their house. Referring to the Thomas Moore poem entitled "'Tis gone and for ever, the light we saw breaking," Marion Walls writes: "What seems to have gone forever for Tressell is Ireland, personified in the character of Barrington, the person to whom he is 'waving a handkerchief' until 'there remained nothing visible.'"

This identification of Barrington with Ireland may be too fanciful, but I could see him as representing Samuel Croker. In terms of the departure of a wealthy man to another world, and waving from the train, I am thinking of Samuel's departure for London circa 1874, when the boy Robert might have waved him off – albeit by boat rather than train. (I also recall the slightly disconcerting discovery I had when, in researching old newspapers for the family of Croker, one of the names which cropped up regularly was a wealthy landowner named Sir Croker Barrington (1817-1890) of Glenstal, Co. Limerick. The house and estate is now a Benedictine monastery and school.)

Robert Tressell, through the voice of Owen, speaks passionately on behalf of children on many occasions in the novel: "And the boy – what hope was there for him?"

And again:

> Often as Owen moodily thought of their circumstances and prospects he told himself that it would be far better if they could all die now, together. He was tired of suffering himself, tired of impotently watching the sufferings of his wife, and appalled at the thought of what was in store for the child.....

Later Owen says:

> No matter how prosperous a man might be, he could not be certain that his children would never want for bread. There were thousands living in misery on starvation wages whose parents had been wealthy people.

When the "loathsome hypocrites" of Mugsborough pretended to sympathise with hungry children but refused to levy proper rates to help the poor, preferring to rely on charity instead, Robert quotes the King James bible: "For I was an hungered and ye gave Me no meat: I was thirsty and ye gave Me no drink: I was a stranger and ye took Me not in: naked and ye clothed Me not." He goes on to describe the plight of the children:

> And meantime, all around them, in the alley and the slum, and more terrible still – because more secret – in the better sort of streets where lived the respectable class of skilled artisans, the little children became thinner and paler day by day for lack of proper food, and went to bed early because there was no fire.

In the light of the questions over the kind of childhood which Robert might have experienced, I believe that the references to children in the novel are very significant. There is compassion, anger and deep concern in Owen's statements about children, and perhaps here we have the voice of the author who was himself acutely aware of what a fractured childhood meant. Owen is unsparing in his condemnation of the effects of the workers' apathy and inertia, and of the effects of their perpetuation of the system that degraded them, going as far as saying that they were the enemies of their own children. Such was the ingrained subservience of the workers that one of them states: "Our children is only like so much dirt compared with the gentry's children and their pleasures are not for the likes of us."

Robert Tressell is now among the immortals and celebrated for his great achievement in writing a novel that is beloved and admired by millions in all parts of the world and that completes its first century in April 2014. As an admirer of Jonathan Swift, Robert may have been familiar with Swift's self-penned epitaph in Latin in St. Patrick's Cathedral, Dublin, although not with W. B. Yeats' poem published in 1933. It serves as an appropriate epitaph for the inimitable Robert Tressell, a writer whose savage indignation also served human liberty.

Hic depositum est Corpus
JONATHAN SWIFT S.T.D.
Hujus Ecclesiae Cathedralis
Decani
Ubi saeva indignatio
Ulterius
Cor lacerare nequit.
Abi Viator
Et imitare, si poteris,
Strenuum pro virili
Libertatis Vindicatorem.

Swift's Epitaph
Swift has sailed into his rest;
Savage indignation there
Cannot lacerate his breast.
Imitate him if you dare,
World-besotted traveller; he
Served human liberty.
(W.B. YEATS)

APPENDIX I:
Croker/Noonan Genealogy

by Fíona Tipple, Family Historian and Member of the Genealogical Association of Ireland.

CROKER Samuel (c.1790 – 1875)

Officer in Constabulary, 1823-1840; Resident Magistrate, Ennis, Co. Clare, until 1 Apr 1843. Died 6 January 1875 at 91 East India (Dock) Road, London.

SPOUSES

QUIN Jane Ussher (~ 1811-1887)
Marriage: 4 September 1827 – Affane
(Waterford, IRELAND)

Offspring
CROKER Samuel (1828-1834)
No known descendants
CROKER Anne Elizabeth (1829-1880)
No known descendants
CROKER Arthur (~ 1832-1900)
SMITH Frances (~ 1836-1896)
4 children: Henry, Mary, Edward and
Thomas
CROKER John Wilson (~ 1834-1903)
FRANKLIN Rebecca (~ 1837-1907)
8 children: Matilda, John, Jane, Rebecca,
Anna, Samuel, Richard and Mary
CROKER Samuel (~ 1836-1889)
JOHNSTON Josephine
No known descendants
CROKER Melian (Minnie) Jane (~ 1844-
1908)
MILLINGTON Richard (~ 1841-1906)
One child: Jane

NOONAN Mary

Offspring
NOONAN Mary Jane (Jennie) (1858-1927)
MEIKLEJON John Bean (1852-1925)
6 children: Edwin, Alice, Ruby, Percival,
Olive and Paul
CROKER Henry John (1860-1935)
MANLEY Kate Eva (1856-1946)
11 children: Ivy, John, Daisy, Mabel, Dorothy,
Marjory, Morris, Harry, Pearl, Ivan and {unk}
CROKER Teresa (1862-)
No known descendants
CROKER Ellie (Zellah) (~ 1866-1946)

MAGUIRE William (~ 1869-1898)
Three children: Francis, William and Leo
CROKER Adelaide Ann (1867-1945)
ROLLESTON —
One child: Arthur
CROKER Robert (1870-1911)
HARTEL Elizabeth (~ 1872-)
One child: Kathleen
CROKER William (1872-)
No known descendants

SAMUEL CROKER TIMELINE

~21

~37

~38

~39

~42

~44

Birth
About 1790 – Ireland – Woodville (Waterford)
Birth of his spouse QUIN Jane Ussher
About 1811
Source: England & Wales, FreeBMD Death
Index, 1837-1915 – Ancestry.com

Marriage with QUIN Jane Ussher
4 September 1827 – Affane (Waterford,
   IRELAND)
Jim Herlihy, p. 108

Birth of his son CROKER Samuel
1828 – Dungarvan (Waterford, IRELAND)

**Birth of his daughter CROKER Anne
Elizabeth**
7 November 1829 – Dungarvan (Waterford,
IRELAND)
This is baptism date – NB
Source: Ireland, Civil Registration Deaths
Index, 1864-1958 – Ancestry.com

Birth of his son CROKER Arthur
About 1832 – ? (IRELAND)
Sources:
England & Wales, FreeBMD Death Index,
1837-1915 – Ancestry.com
1891 England Census – Ancestry.com (Other)
1881 England Census – Ancestry.com (Other)

Birth of his son CROKER John Wilson
About 1834 – Carrick-on-Suir – Tipperary
(IRELAND)
Sources:
1881 England Census – Ancestry.com

1871 England Census – Ancestry.com
1891 England Census – Ancestry.com
England & Wales, FreeBMD Death Index,
1837-1915 – Ancestry.com
Ireland, Census, 1901 – National Archives
of Ireland

~44

Death of his son CROKER Samuel
1834 – Dungarvan (Waterford, IRELAND)
Source:
Tipperary Clan Archive (Waterford Mail, 9
Apr 1834): Burial, Dungarvan, Co. Waterford,
Samuel, eldest son of Samuel [etc.] –
FindMyPast.com

~46

Birth of his son CROKER Samuel
About 1836
Source: Ireland, Civil Registration Deaths
Index, 1864-1958 – Ancestry.com

~54

**Birth of his daughter CROKER Melian
(Minnie) Jane**
About 1844 – ? (IRELAND)
Sources:
1881 England Census – Ancestry.com
1901 England Census – Ancestry.com

~68

**Birth of his daughter NOONAN Mary Jane
(Jennie)**
1858 – Athlone (Westmeath, IRELAND)
Address on baptismal record: Preaching Lane
Sources:
Ireland, Selections of Catholic Parish
Baptisms, 1742-1881 – Ancestry.com
1911 England Census – Ancestry.com
England & Wales, Death Index, 1916-2007 –
Ancestry.com
1901 England Census – Ancestry.com
1891 England Census – Ancestry.com
England & Wales Marriages 1837-2008 –
FindMyPast.com

~70

Birth of his son CROKER Henry John
8 August 1860 – Dublin (Dublin,
IRELAND)
Address on baptismal record: 47
Montgomery Street

Sources:
1891 England Census – Ancestry.com
1901 England Census – Ancestry.com

~72

Birth of his daughter CROKER Teresa

17 February 1862 – Dublin (Dublin, IRELAND)
Source:
Irishgenealogy.ie
Address on baptismal record: 18 Mabbot Street

~76

Birth of his daughter CROKER Ellie (Zellah)

About 1866 – At Sea
Age given as 23 on marriage record. Father named as "Samuel Noonan, pensioner", 1891 and 1911 censuses gives her place of birth as "at sea"
Sources:
Liverpool, England, Marriages and Banns, 1813-1921
1911 England Census – Ancestry.com
1891 England Census – Ancestry.com
Liverpool, England, Catholic Burials, 1813-1988 – Ancestry.com
England & Wales, Death Index, 1916-2007 – Ancestry.com

~77

Birth of his daughter CROKER Adelaide Ann

3 May 1867 – Dublin (Dublin, IRELAND)
Address on baptismal record: 53 Wellington Street
Sources:
Ireland, Civil Registration Births Index, 1864-1958 – Ancestry.com
Ireland, Births and Baptisms, 1620-1911 – Ancestry.com
England & Wales, Death Index, 1916-2007 – Ancestry.com
1911 England Census – Ancestry.com
UK, Outward Passenger Lists, 1890-1960 – Ancestry.com
1891 England Census – Ancestry.com

~80

Birth of his son CROKER Robert
18 April 1870 – Dublin (Dublin, IRELAND)
Address on baptismal record: 37 Wexford Street
Sources:
Ireland, Births and Baptisms, 1620-1911 – Ancestry.com
Liverpool, England, Burials, 1813-1974 – Ancestry.com
Ireland, Civil Registration Births Index, 1864-1958 – Ancestry.com

~82

Birth of his son CROKER William
20 January 1872 – Dublin (Dublin, IRELAND)
Address on baptismal record: George's Place
Sources:
Ireland, Births and Baptisms, 1620-1911 – Ancestry.com
Ireland, Civil Registration Births Index, 1864-1958 – Ancestry.com

~85

Death
6 January 1875 – 91 East India Dock Road, Poplar, London (ENGLAND)
Source:
England & Wales Deaths 1837-2007 – FindMyPast.com
To date no will or administration traced in either Dublin or London.

Edwin

Alice

Ruby

Percival

Olive

Paul
Meiklejon

D. 1894
Sebastian
Zumbuhl

1876 - 1915
39
Sebastian

1878 - 1897
19
Leo

m. 1875

D. 1896
Mary
Noonan

1852 - 1925
73
John
Bean
Meiklejon

1858 - 1927
69
Mary Jane
(Jennie)
Noonan

m. 1875

Ivy

John

Daisy

Mabel

Dorothy

Marjory

Morris

Harry

Pearl

Ivan

?

1860 - 1935
75
Henry John
Croker
(Noonan)

1856 - 1946
90
Kate
Eva
Manley

m. 1883

1862
Teresa
Croker

Francis
William
Leo

1866 - 1946
80
Ellie
(Zellah)
Noonan

1869 - 1898
29
William
Maguire

m. 1892

Arthur

1867 - 1945
78
Adelaide
Ann Croker
(Noonan)

Rolleston

m. Jul 1914

1915 - 2000
85
Joan
Meiklejon

D. 2013
Reg
Johnson

1892 - 1988
96
Kathleen
Noonan

1870 - 1911
40
Robert
Croker
(Noonan)

1872
Elizabeth
Hartel

m. 15 Oct 1891

1872
William
Croker

1790 - 1875
85
Samuel
Croker

m. 4 Sept 1827

Henry

Mary

Edward

Thomas

Matilda

John

Jane

Rebecca

Anna

Samuel Richard

Mary

1828 - 1834
6
Samuel
Croker

1829 - 1880
51
Anne
Elizabeth
Croker

1832 - 1900
68
Arthur
Croker

1836 - 1896
60
Frances
Smith

m. 1866

1834 - 1903
69
John
Wilson
Croker

1837 - 1907
70
Rebecca
Franklin

m. 1857

1811 - 1887
76
Jane
Ussher
Quin

1836 - 1889
53
Samuel
Croker

Josephine
Johnston

m. 1859

1844 - 1908
64
Melian
(Minnie)
Jane Croker

1841 - 1906
65
Richard
Millington

m. 1872

Jane

APPENDIX 2:

Registry of Deeds document of 1873.

Ref: Registry of Deeds. 1873.33.078

No 78. Croker to Noonan. Regd. 16 August 1873 at 40m past 10 c.

To the Registrar appointed by Act of Parliament for registering deeds, wills and so forth in Ireland:

A memorial of a deed of conveyance bearing date the 11th day of August, 1873 and made between Samuel Croker of No 1 Winslow Terrace, Rathgar in the County of Dublin Esq. of the one part and Mary Anne Noonan of No.38 Bessborough Avenue, North Strand in the County of Dublin, spinster, of the other part.

After reciting fee farm grant bearing date the 21st day of November 1859 and made by one Hugh Eccles to one Robert Johnston under the provisions of the Renewable Household Conversion Act and in consideration of a certain lease for lives renewable forever bearing date 25th day of June 1831 of the premises therein and hereinafter particularly described to hold to the said Robert Johnston his heirs and assigns forever at the yearly fee farm rent of £27 13s 10¼ present currency and to the observance and performance of the covenants and agreements wherein contained and after further recitals showing how the interest of the grantee in said grant had become and was then vested in the said Samuel Croker **the deed of which this is a memorial witnessed that in pursuance of and to effectuate the desire wherein mentioned and for the consideration therein the said Samuel Croker granted and conveyed unto the said Mary Noonan her heirs and assigns all that brick house with the back side or garden thereunto belonging situate lying and being in Great Britain St., (now numbered 145) in the parish of St. George and county of the city of Dublin** containing in front to the said street 16feet and in depth from front to rere 91feet be the same more or less bounded on the east by the lane formerly leading to the ground of the Rev. Richard Hopkins but now known as North Great George's Street, on the west by the house wherein the said Richard Hopkins formerly dwelt, on the north by the ground of the said Richard Hopkins and on the south by Great Britain Street and as now in the possession of Edward Wood, merchant and all and singular other the premises comprised in and granted by the said rented(?) fee farm grant and all the right members and appurtenances thereof together with the said indenture and all deeds and writings relating to the title of the same premises now in the custody of the said Samuel Croker to hold unto the said Mary Noonan her heirs and assigns to the use of the said Mary Noonan her heirs and assigns forever subject to the same yearly farm rent and performance and observance of the covenants and agreements therein contained and also subject to the same lease for lives date 1st July 1831 (being the last renewal of the original lease of 30th December 1794) and to all other renewals to be made in pursuance of the covenant in said original lease contained which said deed and this memorial as to the due execution thereof by the said Samuel Croker and as to the due execution of the said deed by the said Mary Noonan are respectively witnessed by W. D. Bradley of 11 Lower Ormond Quay in the city of Dublin, Solicitor and Joseph O'Donoghue of No.1 Dunville Ave., Ranelagh in the County of Dublin, law clerk. ...

The document ends with confirmation of dates and times.
©Property Registration Authority.

APPENDIX 3:

Registry of Deeds document of 1874.

Ref: 1874.33.090.

Croker and ors. to Croker and ors. Regd. 17 Aug 1874. At 17m past 10 c.

A memorial of a deed of family settlement bearing date of 2 June 1874 and made between Samuel Croker at present residing in London in the Co. of Middlesex in England, retired Resident Magistrate of the first part, Jane Ussher Croker of Number 1 Winslow Tce, Rathgar in the County of Dublin, wife of the said Samuel Croker, of the second part Annie Croker of the same place, daughter of the said Samuel Croker, of the third part Arthur Croker, Esq. a Surgeon-Major in Her Majesty's army now stationed at Queenstown in the County of Cork, eldest son of the said Samuel Croker, John W. Croker of 74 Berkeley St. Liverpool in England, 2nd son of the said Samuel Croker, Samuel Croker junior, of Parsonstown in the King's Co. Esq. 3rd son of the said Samuel Croker, and Richard Millington of Number 109 Belgrave Road, Birmingham in England. Esquire and Melian Jane Millington otherwise Croker his wife of the same place, said Melian Jane Millington being another daughter of the said Samuel Croker of the fourth part and the said John Croker a trustee for certain purposes thereinafter mentioned of the fifth part and William David Bradley of Lower Ormond Quay Dublin a trustee for certain other purposes thereinafter mentioned.

Reciting that the said Samuel Croker was entitled to two pensions of £400 and £36 10s for his life and reciting a certain mortgage bearing date 21st November 1865 whereby the Rev. James Macredy in consideration of the sum of £500 paid him by the said Samuel Croker demised to him certain premises therein and herein after particularly described subject to redemption on payment of said sum and interest at 6 per cent and that a sum of £300 with interest from the 1st of December last remained due on foot of said mortgage. And reciting a certain lease dated 1st December 1869 wherein James Hill demised to the said Samuel Croker , certain premises known as No.1 Winslow Tce for a term of 879 years subject to the yearly rent of sixteen pounds and reciting a certain indenture bearing date the 28th day of August 1867 whereby Charles Carter Barrett and others granted unto said Samuel Croker his heirs and assigns certain premises in Great Britain Street and **that by a certain indenture dated the 11th August 1873 the said Samuel Croker granted to one Mary Noonan an annuity of £100 payable out of his said pensions and by another deed of the same date granted to her the said premises in Great Britain St. hereinafter described. And reciting that questions were raised as to the validity of the said two last mentioned deeds and that to settle this and all other differences the memorializing settlement had been entered into.**

The deed of which this is a memorial witnessed that the said Samuel Croker assigned unto the said John Croker, his executors admors and assigns all that the said principal sum of £300 due on foot of said mortgage to hold upon the trusts thereinafter mentioned and the said Samuel Croker did thereby also assign and make over unto the said John Croker his executors admors and assigns all that part of the lands of Irvine and Irvine Castle with its sub-denominations called Clure together with the buildings thereon and all other the premises contained in said indenture of mortgage and all the estate and interest of the said Samuel Croker in the same to hold subject to redemption and after declaring the trusts of the said monies. It is further witnessed that the said Samuel Croker did thereby assign unto the said John Croker his executors admors and assigns all that and those that piece or plot of ground being the lands of Rathgar with the dwelling house erected thereon now known as No.1

Winslow Terrace Rathgar being the premises comprised in and expressed to be demised by the indenture of the 1st day of December 1869 and meared and bounded as therein described and being situate in the barony of Rathdown and County of Dublin and also all and singular the household furniture and effects and ornaments, plate, linen, china, glass and books and other personal chattels of every description then in or about the dwelling house No.1 Winslow Terrace aforesaid and whether the same may or may not be particularly specified in the schedule to said memorializing deed to hold to the said John Croker his executors admors and assigns as to said plot of ground and premises for the residue of the term for which said were held and as to all other premises ——— (?) thereinbefore assigned for the absolute interest therein upon the trusts therein particularly set forth. .

It is further witnessed that the said Samuel Croker did thereby assign and make over unto the said William David Bradley his executors etc the said annual pensions and sum of £400 and £36 10s to hold upon trust to make thereout the payments therein directed to be made and the better to enable the said William David Bradley to recover and receive the said pensions the said Samuel Croker appointed him the said William David Bradley his the said Samuel Croker's true and lawful attorney to demand on(?) for receive and give receipt for the said pensions and to execute and do all such other things as shall be necessary or expedient.

It was further witnessed that all the said parties thereto witnessing themselves respectively and for the respective heirs, executors, admors and assigns ratified and confirmed said two indentures of the 11th day of August 1873 and should any of them commence any legal proceedings whatsoever for the purpose of impeaching said two indentures or take any steps to prevent or hinder the said Samuel Croker from residing where he chose that then the memorializing deed was to cease and be absolutely null and void.

And said deed which was executed in duplicate contained a power given to Jane Usher Croker and Annie Croker and the survivor of them of appointing a trustee in the place of the said John Croker or any trustee appointed in his place. And a power to said Samuel Croker of appointing a trustee in the place of W.D. Bradley or any trustee appointed in his place which said deed and this memorial as to the due execution thereof by the said Samuel Croker are respectively witnessed by P.M. Bray of 130 East India Dock Road, Popla (sic), London, Gentleman and W. G. Bradley of 11 Ormond Quay, Dublin, Solicitor.

And as to the due execution of said deed by the said Annie Croker who signs deed as Anne E. Croker and Samuel Croker junior as witnessed by the said W.G. Bradley and G.H. Cooper of 9 Clare Street in the city of Dublin, solicitor, and as to the due execution of said deed by said Arthur Croker as witnessed by Peter Gready of Queenstown, Superintendent, and said W.G. Bradley and as to the due execution of the said deed by the said Jane Usher Croker, Richard Millington, Melian Jane Millington, John Croker and W.D. Bradley as witnessed by the said W. G. Bradley, solicitor.

Samuel Croker seal signed and sealed by the said Samuel Croker in the presence of P. M. Bray of 130 East India Dock Road, Popla, London, W. G. Bradley solicitor of 11 Ormond Quay, Dublin.

The document ends with confirmation of dates and times.

©Property Registration Authority.

ACKNOWLEDGEMENTS

I have known about the novel *The Ragged Trousered Philanthropists* since my student days, but like many people, I knew only that it was a very long socialist novel. In 2009, while researching my book *Ascend or Die: Richard Crosbie, Pioneer of Balloon Flight in Ireland* (The History Press Ireland, 2010) I came across Robert Tressell's balloon illustrations on-line. Intrigued by Tressell's Irish background, and by some curious similarities between the lives of Crosbie and Noonan, I contacted Reg Johnson, custodian of the Robert Tressell Family Papers, with a request to publish some of Robert's drawings in the book. I thought it appropriate to have the two unheralded and little known Irish heroes together in the book. Reg responded enthusiastically and sent me a copy of Robert's article on "The Evolution of the Airship" as well as some of his balloon images and other photographs. I was very grateful for Reg Johnson's generosity and I became determined to find out more about Robert Tressell, and to make his achievements better known in his native land.

I began by reading *The Ragged Trousered Philanthropists* for the first time, and then the biographies by Fred Ball. Like all Tressell biographers, I am greatly indebted to Fred Ball's persistence and dedication to his search and I was astonished by his discoveries. His two books are the foundations on which this book is built. I first wrote about Robert in a feature article for *The Irish Independent* Weekend Magazine of 10th September 2011 to commemorate the centenary of his death, and I continued to research his life and work. It is a pleasure to be able to add to the information on Robert Noonan's Irish background, continuing the archive explorations of Fred Ball.

I have found Dave Harker's biography very informative, especially as it is written from the perspective of a socialist and trade union activist. The more recent transatlantic co-operation of Julie Cairnie and Marion Walls has also produced a very interesting book. Steve Peak and Trevor Hopper have published books with a focus on Robert's associations with Hastings.

In researching the lives of Samuel Croker and Mary Noonan, I am greatly indebted to the expertise and enthusiasm of Fíona Tipple, who discovered the genealogical details which enabled me to trace their lives in a little more detail. Fíona's advice also led me to the discovery of the details hidden in the Registry of Deeds in Dublin, which might otherwise have been missed. The new family information included here would not have come to light without Fíona's great work. Brenda Douglas, a descendant of Robert Noonan's sister Ellie, has been extremely helpful in providing family information and the wonderful photograph of Mary Noonan.

Pádraig Yeates, author of *Lockout: Dublin 1913* among other books, and secretary of the 1913 Committee, has been very supportive since I first informed him of my research and I am grateful for his advice. Professor Maria Luddy has also been very helpful.

Sadly, when I tried to make contact again with Reg Johnson in the autumn of 2013, I discovered that he had passed away earlier in the year. The Robert Tressell Family Papers are now in the care of the University of Brighton at Hastings and I am grateful for permission to publish images from the archive. I have not been in a position to consult these papers and have relied on the published work of others.

I am very grateful to Ion Castro and Dee Daly of the Robert Tressell Society in Hastings who have been very supportive and who have provided photographs. Steve Peak has very generously allowed the use of images from his website.

The Trades Union Congress website www.unionhistory.info has a great deal of interesting information of Robert Tressell's life and work. It also has the full manuscript of the novel, available to all as Robert wrote it. I am grateful for permission to reproduce images from this source and for the co-operation of Christine Coates of Trades Union Congress Library.

Anne O'Connor, Julia Barrett and Grace Timmins have helped with my research and so has Fr. Donal McCarthy, archivist of the Pallotine Order. My gratitude also to Susan Waine of Ashfield Press. Finally, sincere thanks to my colleagues in Kilmacud-Stillorgan Local History Society whose support has made this publication possible: Julia Barrett, Lyn Lynch, Anne O'Connor, Clive O'Connor, Pat Sheridan and Peter Sobolewski.

Any errors are my own responsibility.

SOURCES

Alfred, David (ed.) *The Robert Tressell Lectures*, 1981-1988 (Workers' Educational Association, 1988)

Ball, F. C. *One of the Damned: The life and times of Robert Tressell, author of The Ragged Trousered Philanthropists* (London, 1973).

Ball, F. C. *Tressell of Mugsborough* (London, 1951)

Boyd, Gary A., *Dublin 1745-1922: Hospitals, Spectacle and Vice* (Dublin, 2006).

Cairnie, Julie and Walls, Marion, (eds.) *Revisiting Robert Tressell's Mugsborough: New Perspectives on The Ragged Trousered Philanthropists* (New York, 2008)

Callan, Charles, *Saothar: Journal of the Irish Labour History Society,* No. 22 (1997) p 113-122.

Dictionary of Irish Biography (2009)

Du Cros, Sir Arthur, *Wheels of Fortune: A Salute to Pioneers* (London, 1938).

Fagan, Terry, *Monto: Madams, Murder and Black Coddle* (Dublin: North Inner City Folklore Project, 2000)

Finegan, John, *The Story of Monto: an account of Dublin's notorious red-light district* (Cork, 1978).

Gollin, Alfred M. *The Impact of Air Power on the British People and Their Government, 1909-1914* (London, 1989).

Harker, Dave, *Tressell: The real story of The Ragged Trousered Philanthropists* (London, 2003)

Hattersley, Roy, "Ragged Edge," *New Statesman,* 10th February 2011.

Herlihy, Jim, *Royal Irish Constabulary Officers: A Biographical Dictionary and Genealogical Guide 1816-1922* (Dublin, 2005).

Hopper, Trevor, *Robert Tressell's Hasting: The Background to 'The Ragged Trousered Philanthropists'* (Fanter Books, 2005)

Hyslop, Jonathan, "A Ragged Trousered Philanthropist and the Empire: Robert Tressell in South Africa," *History Workshop Journal* No. 51 (2001)

Luddy, Maria, *Prostitution and Irish Society, 1800-1940* (Cambridge, 2007)

Meade, Rosie, "More than 'just' a novel: The Ragged Trousered Philanthropists (1914) *Saothar: Journal of the Irish Labour History Society,* No. 34 (2009) p. 145-154.

Miles, Peter, Introduction to Oxford World Classics edition of *The Ragged Trousered Philanthropists* (Oxford, 2005).

Mitchell, Jack, *Robert Tressell and 'The Ragged Trousered Philanthropists'* (London, 1969)

Peak, Steve, *Mugsborough Revisited: Author Robert Tressell and the setting of his famous book 'The Ragged Trousered Philanthropists'* (Hastings, 2011)

Pope, Jessie, Introduction to Penguin (1940) edition of *The Ragged Trousered Philanthropists.*

Prunty, Jacinta, *Dublin Slums, 1800-1925: A Study in Urban Geography* (Dublin 1998 and 2011)

Sillitoe, Alan, Introduction to the Harper Perennial edition of *The Ragged Trousered Philanthropists* (London, 2005).

Swinnerton, Frank, *The adventures of a manuscript: being the story of The Ragged Trousered Philanthropists* (London, 1956)

Registry of Deeds, Henrietta St., Dublin.

DOCUMENTS

1873.30.145.

1873.33.078

1874.33.090.

1875.9.264.

WEBSITES

http://www.hastingschronicle.net/tressell.html. Steve Peak's comprehensive website on the history of Hastings has a section devoted to Robert Tressell.

www.1066.net/tressell/ The website of the Robert Tressell Society. Contains a timeline of Robert's life, many photographs and a visitors' book.

www.unionhistory.info/ragged/ragged/php. The complete manuscript of The Ragged Trousered Philanthropists is available to read on this website which has a wide range of photographs and information provided by Dave Harker. The site also has a link to the full text of Robert Tressell's essay "The Evolution of the Airship."

http://members.iinet.net.au/~nickred/croker_research/The_Irish_CROKER.pdf . Nick Reddan's website on the Croker family.

Dave Harker and Reg Johnson: *A Working Bibliography* (Revised 2008) available on www.unionhistory.info. A comprehensive listing of all material in the Robert Tressell Family Papers, formerly in the care of Reg Johnson and now in the University of Brighton at Hastings.

http://churchrecords.irishgenealogy.ie/churchrecords/details/208b7f0005623: Details of the record of the baptism of Robert Croker.